VOLLEYBALL
Fundamentals

Second Edition

Joel Dearing
Springfield College

HUMAN KINETICS

Library of Congress Cataloging-in-Publication Data

Names: Dearing, Joel, author.

Title: Volleyball fundamentals / Joel Dearing, Springfield College.

Description: Second Edition. | Champaign, Illinois : Human Kinetics, [2018] | Series: Sports Fundamentals Series

Identifiers: LCCN 2018019651 (print) | LCCN 2018019991 (ebook) | ISBN 9781492567301 (ebook) | ISBN 9781492567295 (print)

Subjects: LCSH: Volleyball.

Classification: LCC GV1015.3 (ebook) | LCC GV1015.3 .V65 2018 (print) | DDC 796.325--dc23

LC record available at https://lccn.loc.gov/2018019651

ISBN: 978-1-4925-6729-5 (print)

The web addresses cited in this text were current as of June 2018, unless otherwise noted.

Acquisitions Editor: Diana Vincer; **Managing Editor:** Karla Walsh; **Copyeditor:** Marissa Wold Uhrina; **Proofreader:** Leigh Keylock; **Permissions Manager:** Martha Gullo; **Graphic Designer:** Julie L. Denzer; **Cover Designer:** Keri Evans; **Cover Design Associate:** Susan Rothermel Allen; **Photograph (cover):** Buda Mendes / Getty Images; **Photographs (interior):** © Human Kinetics; **Photo Production Coordinator:** Amy M. Rose; **Photo Production Manager:** Jason Allen; **Senior Art Manager:** Kelly Hendren; **Illustrations:** © Human Kinetics; **Printer:** Versa Press

We thank The High School of St. Thomas More in Champaign, Illinois, for assistance in providing the location for the photo shoot for this book.

Human Kinetics books are available at special discounts for bulk purchase. Special editions or book excerpts can also be created to specification. For details, contact the Special Sales Manager at Human Kinetics.

Printed in the United States of America   10 9 8 7 6 5 4 3 2 1

The paper in this book is certified under a sustainable forestry program.

Human Kinetics

P.O. Box 5076
Champaign, IL 61825-5076
Website: www.HumanKinetics.com

In the United States, email info@hkusa.com or call 800-747-4457.
In Canada, email info@hkcanada.com.
In the United Kingdom/Europe, email hk@hkeurope.com.

For information about Human Kinetics' coverage in other areas of the world,
please visit our website: **www.HumanKinetics.com**

E7313

Contents

Acknowledgments iv

Introduction v

Key to Diagrams x

Chapter 1   **Volleyball Basics** **1**

Chapter 2   **Serving** **9**

Chapter 3   **Receiving the Serve** **21**

Chapter 4   **Setting** **31**

Chapter 5   **Attacking** **47**

Chapter 6   **Blocking** **61**

Chapter 7   **Digging** **75**

Chapter 8   **The Libero** **87**

Chapter 9   **Team Defense** **97**

Chapter 10   **Free Ball** **113**

Chapter 11   **Team Offense** **121**

Chapter 12   **Transition** **135**

Chapter 13   **Modified Games** **145**

Chapter 14   **Scoring Systems** **155**

About the Author 165

Acknowledgments

I would like to thank my Human Kinetics team for getting this second edition to the finish line. This very impressive group of professionals includes Diana Vincer, Cynthia McEntire, Karla Walsh, Amy Rose, Coree Clark, and Jason Allen. With my 40 seasons of coaching and more than 30 years of running summer camps, conducting clinics, and working with the USA Volleyball Coaching Accreditation Program as an instructor, it is impossible to give ample credit for what I know about coaching and teaching volleyball. I want to acknowledge all with whom I shared these experiences—experiences I am now passing on in this book. I was blessed to coach hundreds of wonderful young women and men and work with many talented and dedicated assistant coaches in four different decades. I learned so much from those experiences, and I am particularly proud of so many of you for entering the coaching ranks. Thanks to three longtime assistant coaches and cherished friends, Marcus Jannitto, Kevin Lynch, and Lev Milman, for the countless lessons I learned from you as well as another very special colleague and friend from the Emerald Isle, Mary Lalor. I was very fortunate to have coaches Moira Long, Aylene Ilkson, and Chelsea Barnicle, along with veteran official Wade Dubois, to bounce questions off during the many months spent completing this project. Thanks to each of you, along with all my Springfield College athletic administrators and coaching comrades—you are a special group. I need to acknowledge my parents, Dave and Doris Dearing, for providing so many opportunities for me that allowed me to live my dream of being called Coach. Most importantly, a word to my family: Thank you, Erin Leigh, Kevin, and Ryan for the many, many ways you have supported and shared in my career. My final acknowledgment, to the love of my life, finds me searching for words to adequately express my gratitude. So I will leave you, Diane, with something special that we discovered long ago to share with each other frequently . . . J R I L Y.

Introduction

Learning the fundamentals of volleyball can be great fun. Volleyball is a unique and exciting game that requires solid teamwork and consistent individual execution. Unlike many other team sports, players rotate to different positions on the court, so all players must be prepared to play a variety of roles on the team. At elite levels players may specialize, but beginners and recreational players should learn the basics of all positions.

Before we cover the fundamental skills of volleyball, let's get you started with the rules of the game and some features.

Court and Equipment

The volleyball court is 18 meters from endline to endline and 9 meters from sideline to sideline (figure I.1). The centerline (below the net) divides the court in half. Each team's attack line is three meters from the centerline. A back-row player must stay behind the attack line when jumping to contact a ball that is above the height of the net. Players may initiate the serve from anywhere along the endline.

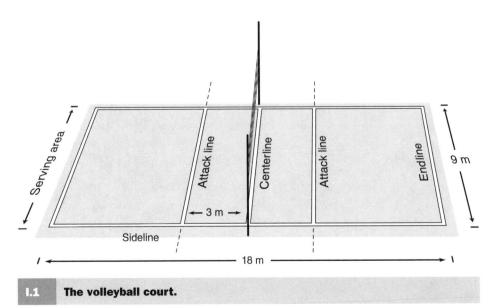

I.1 The volleyball court.

For women's volleyball, the net is 2.24 meters (7 feet, 4-1/8 inches) high; for men's volleyball, the net is 2.43 meters (7 feet, 11-5/8 inches) high. The net should be strung tightly to avoid any sagging and to allow a ball driven into the net to rebound cleanly instead of dropping straight to the floor.

Antennae are connected to the volleyball net just above the sidelines (figure I.2). The volleyball must always pass over the net and between the antennae on a serve and throughout a rally. Safety rules require that the poles and the referee stand must be padded.

Most beginning volleyball players think of each side of the court as two zones: front row and back row. Help your players discover right from the start that there are six zones (figure I.3): right back (zone 1), right front (zone 2), middle front (zone 3), left front (zone 4), left back (zone 5), and middle back (zone 6).

What do you need to play? Begin with volleyball shoes, knee pads, and a volleyball. Choose an indoor or outdoor court. Talk to a local volleyball coach for sound advice on what type of ball to purchase.

The proper uniform includes matching T-shirts and shorts, appropriate volleyball shoes, and knee pads. If you are starting a new team, you will need to purchase T-shirts with numbers on the front and back; then select team shorts. The color and brand should be

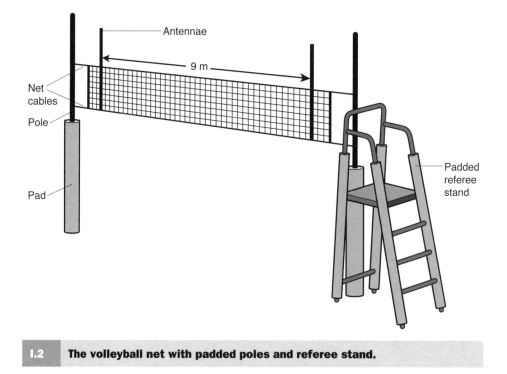

I.2   **The volleyball net with padded poles and referee stand.**

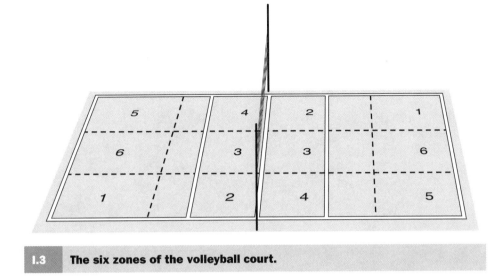

The six zones of the volleyball court.

the same for all players, with the exception of the uniforms worn by liberos (see chapter 8), who are required to wear a shirt of a contrasting color.

Rules

For an indoor six-person game, each team has six players on the court in a predetermined lineup. Prior to the serve, players must be in their legal positions, relative to any adjacent player, to avoid an overlap penalty. Each zone has two to three adjacent players, as shown by the arrows in figure I.4. An overlap violation would be called, for example, if at the moment of service the middle back player is closer to the centerline than the middle front player or if the middle back player is closer to the left sideline than the left back player. (See chapters 9 and 11 for more about legal defensive and offensive formations.) Once the server contacts the ball, players may change positions for the remainder of the rally. Back-row players may play near the net but may not block or attack a ball that is above the height of the net.

A legal serve may contact the net but must cross over the net and between the antennae. A server who steps on the endline prior to contact is considered in the court, resulting in a serving fault.

The receiving team must return the ball to the other side of the net within three team contacts, and no individual may contact the ball more than once consecutively. An individual or group block does not

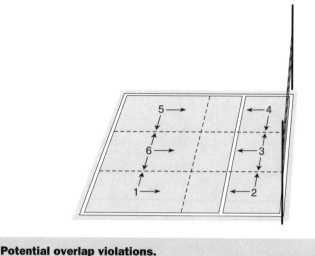

count as a contact for any player; a player is allowed to block and then make another legal contact with the ball.

Throughout a rally, the ball must cross the net between the antennae. Any ball that lands on a sideline or endline is considered in bounds. Players may not touch the net. Each time the receiving team wins a rally, the players on that team rotate one position in a clockwise direction.

Rally scoring is a system in which a point is scored on every play. Rally scoring replaced the traditional scoring method, which awarded points only to the serving team. See chapter 14 for more information on scoring systems, including some unique ways to keep track of the score during drills.

In an outdoor beach or grass-court game, players typically play two versus two. The outdoor game provides the additional challenges of playing in the sun and wind. To minimize the advantage of playing on a particular side of the court (e.g., the side with less glare), the two teams change sides after every 7 points in sets 1 and 2 and after 5 points in a deciding set 3. The basic skills (serve, pass, set, attack, block, and dig) are the same for outdoor volleyball.

In contrast to the blocking rule for indoor volleyball, in the beach game, a block does count as an individual and team contact. The outdoor game utilizes a slightly smaller court (8 meters by 16 meters) with no attack line, so players can attack from anywhere on the court.

Substitutions

The rules regarding substitution limits differ greatly between high school games and international games. For instructional classes, it is probably best to limit the maximum number of players on the court to six.

My introduction to volleyball during junior high school was the nine-per-side game. The rotation pattern was a zigzag across the back row, then across the middle, and finally to the front row. Avoid this at all costs. If more than six players are on a team, simply place substitutes off the court near zones 4 and 2 (figure I.5). Players rotate from zone 1 to zone 6 to zone 5, then leave the court for one play, and then return to zone 4. Players then rotate from zone 4 to zone 3 to zone 2 and then step off again for a play before going back to serve.

Understanding these rules provides a solid foundation of knowledge that will assist you as you build your game. Let's continue the construction with the basics in chapter 1.

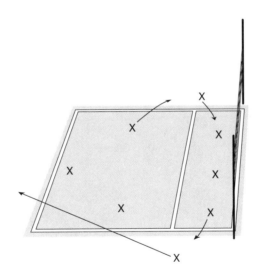

I.5   **Substitution pattern when there are more than six players.**

Key to Diagrams

S	Server
T	Target
△	Cone
→	Player movement
---→	Ball movement
▱	Ball cart
Ts	Tosser
P	Passer
●	Volleyball
⊗	Bonus ball
C	Coach/instructor
⌷C	Coach on a box
St	Setter
X	Player
Xc	Ball collector
A	Attacker
L	Left-handed player
R	Right-handed player
B	Blocker
F	Female player
M	Male player
D	Digger/defender
⑦ ⑩	Setter/right-side player
◈8 ◈11	Left-side player
9 12	Designated middle
△L or △13	Libero

CHAPTER

Volleyball Basics

The opportunity to refresh this book with a second edition has allowed and challenged me to consider how best to provide practical and foundational information to help you learn to play this great game. I continue to carve out time to work on individual fundamentals with new learners of the sport. At times, this means isolating skill development with drills designed to provide some repetitions.

In chapters 2 to 7, you will discover skill keys (words and phrases to focus on) as you learn each of the six basic fundamental skills: serving, passing, setting, attacking, blocking, and digging. Think of these keys as your tools. As a coach, I settled on particular words and phrases to use both with my team in practice and with aspiring players in clinics and camps. Whenever and wherever I teach volleyball skills, my objective is to focus my feedback on one key at a time.

To receive the greatest benefit from working on fundamentals, I suggest that you focus on one skill at a time, performing the entire skill whenever possible. Even accomplished players who want to take their game to another level benefit from taking the time to focus heavily on the execution of a skill, such as an experienced setter establishing a goal of jump setting 100 percent of the time. Part of that training process might include drills and activities that simply allow the player to get a feel for repetitive jump setting, while receiving video and specific feedback one key at a time.

For you, this might mean working on a rather simple change in transferring body momentum as you serve, if you discover that your last step is with your dominant foot. You will see the phrase "step with the nondominant foot" in the next chapter. Watch a softball or baseball pitcher: a righty steps with the left foot during the throw, while a lefty steps forward with the right foot. The same holds true for serving. As you look at the keys for serving, you may want to take time to serve repetitively and focus on your last step, but be sure you fully execute the serve. Worry less about the contact and result, while really focusing on feeling yourself stepping in opposition. Early in your learning process, taking the time to serve in succession, and not immediately entering the court to play defense, may be the best use of your time.

Intentional decisions, however, need to be made for the healthy philosophical tension that exists between training fundamental skills and the ever popular approach of using game-like (experiential learning) opportunities to teach the game. In both educational and competitive teaching situations, I have challenged myself to guide learners as often as possible through progressions of activities, adjusted as needed to become increasingly game-like for the participant.

I had a unique opportunity as a professor in our physical education preparation program at Springfield College to develop teaching strategies for future teachers of junior high–level volleyball units that essentially used 3v3 activities exclusively in every lesson. That approach placed the emphasis on allowing the game to teach the game. I wrestled with planning variations of 3v3 play to introduce beginners to the basic skills while simulating the sequences of contacts that represent how the game is actually played. Skill keys still needed to be introduced, and feedback to participants on those keys still needed to be provided.

The benefit derived from this approach is that new learners always got a feel for the game. The net was involved 100 percent of the time, which provided ongoing experiences for students to respond to the ball, their own teammates, and the opponents in the two most central objectives in the game: (1) the need to return the ball over the net and (2) the need to keep the ball off the floor.

Combining these types of teaching experiences in a physical education setting with 40 seasons of preparing practice plans daily to challenge highly competitive collegiate players informed the decisions I have made with the content of this book.

I have found—and continue to find—each drill in this book helpful to all players, regardless of where they are on the learning continuum. You will notice a wide variety of strategies for how each drill is initiated, along with variations on how you can take the activity to the next level. You'll find drill instructions that provide a number of game-like methods. The sooner you get to drills where players are initiating a rally, the better. One thing I know from over 30 years of instruction: people love to play this sport. With that in mind, here are some volleyball basics to get you started.

Reading

An often overlooked skill is reading, which I operationally define as the ability to anticipate and react to what is about to happen next on the court. One of the benefits of game-like drills is the constant opportunity to develop your reading skills. Each rally provides differences (subtle or drastic) in the body positions (in contact with the floor or in the air) of competitors about to contact the ball and in the angle, trajectory, and speed of the ball as it crosses the net.

I have observed that for some players, reading seems to be a sixth sense. When exhibited expertly, reading is, among other things, a combination of focus, awareness, concentration, and competitive attitude. The first three attributes vary between individuals and over the course of a practice session or match, but levels of competitiveness are largely determined by motivation.

Moving into the realm of sport psychology is beyond the scope of this book, but you will notice in many drills and activities that scoring and a scoreboard are included. You get to determine your level of competitiveness, and a scoreboard will help. Plus, it won't take long for you to discover the pure joy that happens when someone makes a great play. Often what makes those plays great is the improbability factor. How did she get to that ball? How did he keep that off the floor? The odds are high that this "great moment" started with the player reading and reacting to the situation.

Reading starts with your eyes. Take a quick peek ahead at chapter 6 (Blocking) for a guide on what to watch when playing defense. The eye sequence outlined there will help you expand your vision capabilities beyond just tracking the ball. As a defender, you need to be able to respond to the direction of approach from opposing attackers. Are they running straight at the net or using an angled approach? Once they jump, take note of the direction their shoulders are facing, and move to defend that part of your court. Your ability to pick up on these types of cues will increase your skill in predicting where the ball is going. Great moments come from players who know where they need to be to keep the ball off the floor.

Communication

Communication is the key to successful team play and your development, both technically (with fundamental skills) and tactically (how to play the game). To grasp and understand the importance of talking as you play, I offer this simple rule: talk before you contact the ball. Players compete in a very congested area. The ball moves quickly, and as I just mentioned, reading and reacting are essential to this game. Effective teams have players who constantly react to the ball and to each situation using communication skills. You will be presented throughout this book with tips on just what to say as you play your way through every rally.

If it is important for all players to talk, then it is equally important for teammates to listen and react to the signals given by their teammates. While verbal communication is of utmost importance, you will discover as you explore this book how nonverbal skills (hand signals, for example) are also commonly used by more experienced players in a variety of ways.

All of this will take time. Start by consistently calling "mine" before contacting the ball, and in short order, this new habit will become more comfortable and have a contagious effect on your teammates. Here is a universal (and, I would suggest, indisputable) volleyball truth: talking leads to movement.

Movement

As you learn the fundamentals of volleyball, you will recognize the need to move constantly on the court. The game of volleyball has a flow. Often players become spectators on the court rather than staying in the flow.

Being ready to move starts with being in a ready body position but also is determined by each part of a rally. Your ready position will depend on a number of factors, including whether you are (1) in the front row or back row, (2) on offense or defense to start a play, or (3) in the middle of the rally and going from one responsibility to the next.

As you anticipate the ball coming across the net and are in the ready position, you should be low enough to move in any direction with your hands apart. Your base of support will vary depending on how you need to move. Volleyball requires short bursts of speed (two or three sprinting steps) and quick shuffle steps in all directions.

Additionally, front-row players need to be in a ready position to complete sequences of steps and movements toward, away from, and along the net. The block, dig, and attack drill (figure 12.3) will push you to work on efficiently moving away from the net after blocking to a position behind the attack line, where you immediately come right back to the net as an attacker. You will also discover photos such as figure 6.6 in chapter 6, Blocking, to help you develop and refine footwork patterns to use when you move laterally along the net as a blocker.

As you gain experience and use the movement-related instruction found in this book, you will discover that not only is an effective ready position needed, but you also need to arrive at your destination ready to touch the ball in a variety of ways and locations.

I remember listening to Doug Beal, former USAV executive director and USA Men's National Team coach, talk about how he evaluates players. He likes to watch what players do between contacts. Effective players are active between contacts. They anticipate what might happen next and move on the court in a low position, expecting the ball to come to them. That is sound advice for you to start with.

Your movement efficiency and effectiveness will increase over time, and you'll find that the key to success is making connections between reading, communication, and movement. Throughout this book, skill keys and drills will be provided to highlight the situations where these important intangibles are needed.

Arm Swing

Pay attention to the helpful hints related to arm swing in the serving and attacking chapters. The simple throwing motion you may have used in other sports may help you develop the whip-like arm action needed in volleyball. Developing the proper mechanics for your arm swing will serve you well.

A combination of forces will be needed as you develop your arm swing, including the potential torque available from your core. You will discover that shoulder rotation and twisting of your torso, for example, will be part of your arm swing for serving or attacking. In many cases, the end product of those movements will lead to another volleyball basic: hitting with topspin.

Topspin

I can't remember how the first volleyball spike I ever witnessed was delivered. I can remember my first impression of the ball being pounded, so I presumed the player used a fist. I was not alone in that presumption because I have seen hundreds of new learners take their first swing just that way. Later in the book we'll discuss the correct way to spike.

To get you on the right path for success, picture your dominant hand open and in the shape of the volleyball. Creating topspin is best achieved by contacting the back of the ball up high with a hand that covers as much of the surface as possible. If pictures are worth a thousand words, then see figure 1.1 and begin now to think about adding a slapping sound when your hand contacts the ball. If you hear a thud, the heel of your hand was likely the point of contact, which often results in an attack or serve sailing out of bounds.

Since we want the ball to come off the hand and go down into the court, this idea of topspin makes a lot of sense. Traditionally, the idea of a wrist snap seems helpful, and you might find that it is; however, research has indicated that the hand isn't in contact long enough with the ball for the time it takes to snap your wrist. So my advice is to take advantage of this era of multicolor balls used at most levels of competition and let the ball provide feedback for you. Watch the ball for forward spin as you start to play the game, and begin to take note of what your hand felt like on the ball when you

1.1   **Open hand to create topspin.**

were successful in creating topspin. More helpful hints on topspin are ahead in the chapters on serving and attacking.

Righties and Lefties

Volleyball terminology includes references to the strong side and weak side. The easiest way to understand these terms is to think about a right-handed player attacking a ball near the left antenna. As it approaches the attacker from a set, the ball arrives at the attacking arm without crossing the player's body (see figure 1.1). The opposite is true if the right-handed player is attacking the ball near the right antenna. As it approaches the attacker from a set, the ball must go past the body to arrive near the attacking arm.

For right-handed players, the left side of the net is their strong or power side and the right side of the net is their weak side. For lefties, the right side of the net is the strong side and the left side of the net is the weak side. Lefties are referred to as "opposites" since they are often placed opposite the setter in the rotation.

Several volleyball skills will be taught without reference to righties or lefties. Footwork patterns associated with serving and attacking will be presented in chapters 2 and 5 with important distinctions suggested for right- and left-handed players.

Left-handed players are often naturals for the setter and opposite positions since the right side of the net is their power side. Lefties who are excited about taking their game to the next level should attempt to play those positions.

Looking Ahead

If you have already started to play volleyball, you may be on the hunt for confirmation of what you have started to learn. You also may have arrived here looking for clarification or clues to help you take your next steps. Let me highlight a few key concepts that you might want to preview or make note of.

- *The W formation.* Chapter 10 outlines one of the most basic situations you will encounter: receiving a free ball. Ball control skills take time to develop. When a team does not gain enough control of the ball in their first two contacts to set up an attack, they are left with only one option: get that third and final team contact over the net to keep the rally alive. Any easy ball coming back over the net to your team is called a free ball. You will discover in figure 10.1 how your team can create and use a W formation each time this scenario occurs.

- *Attacking.* Attacking is exhilarating and a great place to start because almost everyone loves the idea of hovering above the net and slamming the ball to the court. I think every clinic I have conducted in the last decade without exception has started with attacking because it is fun and there is no quicker way to get smiles on faces. If you head off to chapter 5 right away, you will find steps to success relating to footwork patterns as you approach the net. Also, be sure to consider the off-speed options (tips and roll shots) that you will want (and need) to add to your arsenal.

- *Defense.* "What a save!" How many times did I hear that from my teams' fans in response to an incredible defensive play that probably drew the biggest ovation of the match? Perhaps that is the part of the game that has drawn you into this sport. Well, take a deeper dive into chapter 7 (Digging) to get an idea on how to safely leave your feet when necessary to keep the ball alive. Unfamiliar with a run-through, a pancake, or a J-stroke? Not after reading this chapter. Plus, peek ahead to chapter 8 on the libero, and you can be a defensive wizard in no time at all.

- *Transition.* Have you ever gotten into one of those long rallies where time after time—just when you thought you had won or lost the point—someone kept the play alive? The continuous shift from offense to defense in those epic battles is called "transition." As you work through the chapters on team systems of play, you will end up in chapter 12, which will equip you with a better understanding of how to move, function, and flow on the court during those hotly contested rallies.

Time to Play

Volleyball, like all sports, has its own etiquette and protocol. For example, competitive volleyball matches allow only the court captain and coach to communicate with the officials, and that communication is limited primarily to calling time-outs or requesting substitutions. Before a match begins, teams indicate they are ready for competition by lining up on the endline and waiting for the official's signal to enter the court and prepare for the first serve.

It's time to turn our attention to the fundamental skills you will need when you take your game to the court. Now, go ahead; you're ready for the first serve. Off to the endline!

Serving

Tom Hay, former Springfield College volleyball coach, often reminded his players, "You can't score if you can't serve." You may think this phrase had more meaning before traditional scoring was replaced by rally scoring. However, one could argue that it is even more important now, since a missed serve not only eliminates a chance for your team to score but also gives your opponent a point plus the right to serve.

Although in competitive situations the server does not communicate prior to contact, the coach may signal the server to serve to a specific zone. Serving strategy often targets the opponent's weakest receiver or the gap between two players. Therefore, serving with control is important. Players with booming serves or spectacular jump serves demonstrate that power is also important. Teachers of sport skills often struggle with the debate over power versus control. This chapter emphasizes both. An effective server needs to develop both a powerful serve and the ability to serve to a specific zone.

Overhead Floater

To execute an overhead floater serve, stand comfortably with your nondominant foot slightly forward. Be sure that your weight is on your back foot. Hold the ball with your nonserving hand out in front of your serving shoulder. Place your serving arm in what coaches often call a "high draw" position with your elbow bent about 90 degrees and above shoulder height (figure 2.1*a*).

Common teaching keys for serving include (1) step, (2) toss (lift) the ball, (3) accelerate hand to ball, and (4) make contact. For the step, simply slide your front foot forward, and you will feel your body weight shift from your back foot to your front foot. As you step forward, toss (or essentially lift) the ball directly in front of your serving shoulder high enough to force you to reach fully as you prepare to contact the ball with your serving hand (figure 2.1*b*).

The toss requires a lot of attention because many errors result from inconsistent height and location of the toss. An important point of emphasis will be to keep the height of your toss near the height of your reach. For the standing floater serve, think about lifting or placing the ball to avoid the common mistake of tossing too high. As you toss the ball, you will use an arm swing to accelerate your hand to the ball, which creates power.

An effective arm swing has a whip-like action. The arm swing begins as you draw your elbow back and above shoulder height, then forward with your contact hand open and palm facing out. Your elbow should remain above the height of your shoulder throughout the whip-like action.

Make sure to reach high and in front as you make contact with an open hand (figure 2.1*c*). To assist in effective contact with a float serve, keep your wrist firm throughout contact with the fingers slightly spread apart to allow your hand to contact more of the surface of the ball, and contact the ball with the meaty part of the serving hand in the center of the ball.

The floater serve is most effective when follow-through is limited. A long and full follow-through may generate too much power, causing the serve to travel out of bounds. You will need to experiment with the timing related to accelerating your hand to the ball and then, upon contact, allowing your serving hand to decelerate and lower naturally to your side. Limiting the follow-through helps provide the floating movement of the serve as it travels to the opponent. This movement is often compared to a knuckleball.

2.1 (a) Step, (b) toss (lift) the ball, (c) accelerate hand to ball.

More to choose and use

The sequence of the toss and contact should be rapid. Remember, the serving hand is accelerating to the ball. As soon as the ball is tossed, the whip-like action or throwing motion of the arm must follow. I believe that rhythm can be effective in some aspects of teaching volleyball skills. I often observe beginner servers tossing the ball extremely high. Generally speaking, the higher the toss, the more difficult it may be for servers to make solid contact. I often provide rhythm-related feedback in this situation by saying, "Toss [pause, pause, pause, pause] hit" repeatedly to mirror the timing they are using with a higher toss than needed. Then, I would offer a new rhythm for them to attempt: "Toss [pause] hit." In these teaching situations, I simply ask, "What would need to happen to your toss to change your rhythm?" The amount of time between the words in these two examples would be reflected in changing from a high toss with a significant delay in contact after releasing the ball to a toss that is quickly followed by a contact.

STEPPING INTO THE SERVE

Many players take several steps prior to serving. Generally, taking more than one step does not provide any advantage. The final step forward with the nondominant foot provides enough transfer of weight. Having said that, watching hundreds of first-year players step onto my college court over the course of 30 years, you can imagine how many variations of serving technique I observed. Now and then, I would see a rocket of a serve from players who took three or four steps as part of their routine. Apart from establishing a consistent starting point to avoid foot faults, I left well enough alone, and some of those players led our team in serving aces.

ROUTINE

The serve, as coaches often remind players, is the one skill where a lot less outside influence exists to affect execution. Servers are introducing the ball to a rally, and players typically develop (or fall into) a routine that includes bouncing the ball a number of times. At times, they need our help finding one that works. Coaches should not underestimate the impact of match management and specialized players on serving performance. At some competitive levels, a three-ball system is utilized. While this speeds up play, we need to recognize the impact on the routine for our servers and simulate that in our practice sessions. Place a ball cart at the end of each court and have players not in the drill stationed at each cart to quickly bounce a ball to the next server.

Additionally, while players will likely benefit in practice from some repetitive serving drills, when they take their game to the competitive court, the "all-around" players who never leave the court will move in and out of their turns to serve every six rotations. Back-row specialists, however, will serve, compete for three rotations, substitute off to stand on the sideline and cheer for three rotations, then sprint to the substitution zone and back onto the court to serve. Keeping these situations in mind, remember as you enter the serving zone and get the ball in your hands to develop a consistent routine that will over time become second nature.

UNDERHAND SERVE

The underhand serve (figure 2.2) is another option as a beginning serve. It does not provide a lot of power, but it can be very accurate and consistent. The rules of volleyball require a toss or release of the ball prior to the serve. Coordination of the toss and contact of an underhand serve is actually quite challenging. Think of the toss in the underhand serve as a release. Create a pendulum motion with your arms. As the hand holding the ball drops, your serving hand moves forward through the ball. Contacting an underhand serve consistently can be difficult. Keep the fingers of your serving hand pointing behind your body to expose the heel of your hand to the ball. This will allow you to contact the ball with the meaty part of your hand. Many players attempt to use a fist for an underhand serve, but this often causes inconsistent contact. In addition, the open hand leads to a more natural progression from the underhand serve to the overhand floater.

2.2 **Underhand serve:** *(a)* **step and swing,** *(b)* **release and contact.**

TOPSPIN SERVE

The primary advantage of developing a topspin serve is power. The topspin serve can provide additional power but requires a few changes from the overhead floater serve. One major change is that the topspin serve requires a full throwing motion and follow-through. Additionally, as introduced in chapter 1, creating topspin requires a contact with your hand covering as much of the surface of the ball as possible. An effective float serve often sounds like a thud, while your topspin contact needs to sound like a slap. Contacting above the center of the back of the ball (figure 2.3) will also be helpful in creating a forward spin on the ball as it crosses the net. You may find it helpful to experiment with a slightly higher toss, but remember to accelerate your hand to the ball and keep your serving elbow above the height of your shoulder throughout the arm swing.

2.3 Topspin contact.

JUMP SERVE

Go for the gold as you bring the heat with either your jump float serve (see figure 2.4a through 2.4c) or a jump topspin serve (see figure 2.5a through 2.5c). The jump serve can be a tremendous weapon; it is both powerful and deceptive. The jump serve can create apprehension in your opponents if they are not used to facing this type of serve. You may find the jump serve easier to develop after you've mastered attacking (chapter 5). In essence, the jump serve is an attack from the endline. Instead of attacking a set from a teammate, you will attack your own toss of the ball. Hold the ball with your dominant hand in front of your serving shoulder as you prepare to run toward the endline. Most players feel more comfortable tossing the ball with the dominant hand of the serving arm. The placement of the toss needs to be high and well in front of you, as you will actually be chasing the

2.4   Jump float: *(a)* approach, *(b)* toss, *(c)* contact.

ball. Notice the sequence in figure 2.5*a* through 2.5*c*. You will launch yourself into the air to contact the ball you tossed high and out in front of you. It is essential you coordinate the toss with a sequence of steps, allowing you to jump and swing naturally. To accomplish this, if you are right-handed, step forward on your dominant foot as you toss the ball (e.g., right foot steps as right hand tosses the ball), and then complete the sequence by chasing the ball with a three-step (left, right, left) finish. Watch elite players with a jump spin serve, and typically they are landing several feet inside the court.

2.5 **Jump topspin:** *(a)* toss, *(b)* approach, *(c)* contact.

At the competitive level, serving strategy is based on your philosophy for playing the game. Will you be conservative or assertive? What are the risks and rewards involved in each situation? You need to answer these types of questions when you take it to the court.

Serving strategy often means serving to a particular zone of your opponent's court. Be sure you can identify the zones of the court as you look across the net (see figure I.3). Initial serving strategy includes the following objectives:

- Serving to the opponent's weakest receiver
- Serving between two players
- Serving short (near or in front of the opponent's attack line)
- Serving to the deep third of the opponent's court

Notice that the first three involve the need for serving control and the final objective requires serving power.

The team's or coach's philosophy also will affect serving strategy, as does level of play. Highly skilled players can control the ball on offense and attack at a high rate of efficiency. Strong, effective serves are needed to force an opponent into poor ball control, leading to a less successful attack from the opponent. At a lower or intermediate level, effective serving may require a high percentage of serves simply to be in play since the opponent's offense may not be overpowering.

Here are some additional serving strategies:

- Serve to the opponent's front-row attackers. Challenge the opponent's strongest attacker to pass the ball, then attack.
- Develop a philosophy of serving, taking into consideration those times when it may be critical not to miss a serve—set point, match point, after an opponent's service error, after your team misses a serve, and immediately following a time-out.
- If the setter has to move from their legal court position to the net, serve into the setter's path, causing them to react to the ball while moving. Ideally, you would like to disrupt the setter or make the setter play the ball.
- Establish a consistent routine prior to contacting the ball that includes your focus on where you want to direct your serve and your steps and toss.

"CLASSIC" (CONTROL) TARGET SERVING

For successful, consistent serves, practice serving for control and accuracy. Along the sidelines, set up cones at the attack line, midway between the attack line and endline, and at the endline (figure 2.6). Six players per court may participate. Three servers line up behind the attack line. Three players line up behind the attack line on the other side of the net to act as targets. The targets keep their hands above their heads to give each server a visual target. The servers serve the ball to their targets, who catch the serves and roll the balls back to the servers. After five successful serves from the attack line, the servers move back to the next cone. After five successful serves there, they move back to the endline. After completing five successful serves from the endline, the servers and targets switch sides and roles.

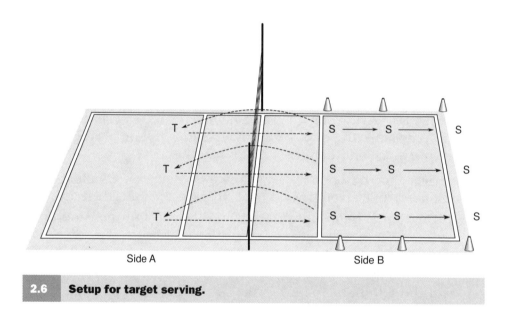

2.6 **Setup for target serving.**

"CLASSIC" (POWER) SERVE DEEP

To practice serving for power with the emphasis on accelerating the hand to the ball, use this activity. On each side of the net along the sidelines, place cones midway between the attack line and endline and at the endline. The cones on side A provide a deep-court target zone for the servers. On side B, 12 servers form 3 lines at the first cone (figure 2.7). The first server in each line attempts to serve deep into the opponent's court, then chases the serve and returns to the back of the line. After each server attempts five serves from the first cone, the servers line up behind the second cone and begin serving from behind the endline.

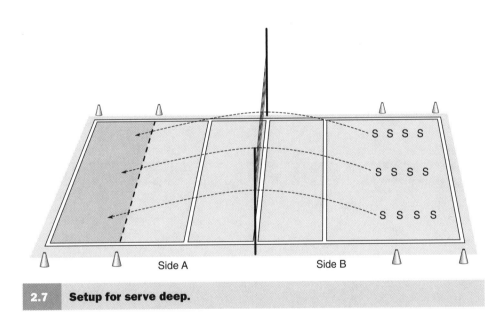

Side A   Side B

2.7 Setup for serve deep.

ZONE SERVING

Using the six zones of the court, outline one or more zones of the court on side A with small cones, and have three to six players on side B quickly alternate serving to the outlined zones for a two-minute time period (figure 2.8). Three to six players during the first two-minute period will collect the balls. Servers can keep track of their successful serves to create a little competition. After two minutes, the servers and collectors change roles.

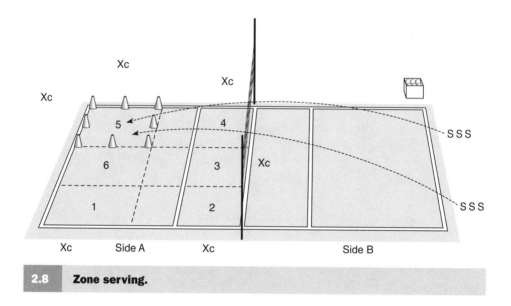

2.8   Zone serving.

Receiving the Serve

The three-contact rule is unique to volleyball. It was not one of the original rules of the game but appeared early in the sport and was first developed in the Philippines. Let's look at these contacts one at a time, beginning with the first contact or touch by the receiving team.

One of the primary skills used to receive the serve is a forearm pass, an action commonly referred to in our sport as "passing." Just as volleyball rules continue to change, so too our jargon has changed. At one point, using the forearms to pass the ball was more commonly referred to as "bumping." Certainly in the 1970s and 1980s, at most levels of volleyball, if a player attempted to receive a serve with an overhead setting motion, the whistle would blow accompanied by a hand signal for a lift or double contact. The exclusivity during that time period of using a forearm pass to receive the serve created one of the first and toughest challenges for those teaching the game: helping new players gain some competency in developing a skill that felt foreign in every way. A significant rule change allowing double contacts (including the use of hands) on any first team contact created, in the minds of many, a more user-friendly game.

This rule change led to a significant shift in ball control tactics by coaches. A second technical and tactical option, now commonly employed to receive a serve, can be described as overhand passing.

In either case, the objective of the first touch in a serve reception system is to control the ball and redirect the serve to a target.

Receiving the serve is often considered the most critical skill in the game. Without an effective pass, it is very difficult to execute your offense. As you begin to practice passing skills, it's important that you always practice passing to a target (whether that is a designated setter or area near the net) and use communication skills ("mine" or "ball") at the same time.

Forearm Pass

To receive a serve and execute a forearm pass successfully, you need to move your feet in response to the serve, create a platform with your arms (keeping your arms away from your body), and contact the ball while in a relatively low athletic stance. Having said that, and while the following description can assist you in developing your passing skills, perhaps a disclaimer is in order.

One of the volleyball basics introduced in chapter 1 related to the tension between teaching fundamentals and allowing the game to teach the game. If we watch the greatest players on the planet receive a serve with their forearms—and, in fact, compare freeze-frame photos of their body at ball contact throughout a match—we are likely to see a variety of body and arm positions. Mastery of this and many fundamental skills will be enhanced as you get to respond to experiential learning opportunities. The teaching keys for passing include (1) move feet to ball, (2) create platform, (3) contact on forearms, and (4) freeze to target.

Prior to the serve, players on the receiving side of the net need to be in a ready-to-move position with feet at least shoulder-width apart, knees bent, and hands apart. You need to move the moment the ball is served and react to the direction and speed as it travels toward your side of the net. A common phrase you'll hear from coaches is "feet to ball." Even though the serve is intercepted with your forearms, moving your feet is often the key to success in passing.

Keep your shoulders forward and arms out in front of you as you move to receive the serve (figure 3.1a). Do not move with your hands together. You will discover that you will be able to move more quickly

3.1 (a) Move feet to ball, (b) create platform, (c) contact on forearms, (d) freeze to target, (e) contact outside of body line.

and efficiently with your hands apart. Use shuffle steps in all directions in response to the serve while remaining in a slightly staggered stance with both knees bent comfortably and shoulders forward.

As you complete your movement, bring your hands together with thumbs and wrists touching to create a platform (figure 3.1b). Simply grab one hand with the other and straighten your arms to prepare to contact the ball. The key is for the arms to work as a platform, rebounding the served ball to the target. When first learning, you may struggle to have the ball contact your arms consistently above the wrists and below the elbows (figure 3.1c). Be patient. Some sports refer to hand-eye coordination; passing requires development of arm-eye coordination.

In most cases, the legs remain stable throughout the contact, although with soft or short serves, some leg drive will assist in pushing the pass toward the target. In this scenario, it is helpful to imagine the amount of leg drive needed to stand up from sitting on the very front edge of a folding chair.

Use every cue possible to predict where the server will direct the ball. The server may look to a zone of your court, or the server's foot may point in that direction.

Your objective when you pass the served ball is to guide the ball to the target, a designated setter who is responsible for setting to available attackers. Through trial and error, you will discover that if you contact the bottom of the ball and swing your arms with a lot of force, the ball will rebound high to the rafters. Focus on getting your platform to contact the back of the ball to correct this error.

"Freeze to the target" is our final fundamental key to emphasize that you need to finish with your platform aimed at your target (figure 3.1d).

In one way, having four or even five players with first contact responsibility may increase a team's chances of not letting a serve hit the floor, but it also creates a lot of seams between players, and for each seam, teammates need to decide quickly who is taking the ball.

If fewer players on the court are assigned to receive the serve, there are now fewer seams but more ground for each of them to cover. As your court space responsibility increases, it is much more likely that you will contact many balls outside of your body line (figure 3.1e). Game-like drills and activities will enable you to learn what it takes on any given serve to make adjustments with your platform to successfully push that first team contact to your designated setter.

PRAYING

A common error inexperienced players commit is referred to as praying. Prior to contact, the player brings joined hands up near the forehead (praying position), then drops the arms near waist level to contact the ball. Players are often unaware they make this mistake and find it hard to correct.

How do you correct this error—or any error, for that matter? Often a technical error can be corrected by taking a look at the step just prior to the repeated error. I heard this tip on error correction many years ago from Sally Kus and have always remembered it as a guide to correcting mistakes. Sally is credited with more than 1,000 coaching victories with the Buffalo (New York) Cheetah volleyball club program. Imagine the number of days in practice she needed to correct players.

To avoid praying when passing, create your platform with long arms and keep your arms extended through contact (figure 3.1*b*). If your arms stay extended, they can't bend, and if they can't bend, you won't develop the habit of praying before you pass.

RECEIVING A SERVE WITH THE HANDS

As noted earlier, a rule change resulted in more players receiving the serve with their hands (figure 3.2). Current rules allow a double contact on any first team contact, including the use of the hands. The previous rule allowed double contact of any first team contact with the exception of hand contact. Although the intent of the rule may have been to give defenders a little more latitude against over-powering attacks, the result has been a tremendous increase in the use of the hands to receive the serve. Some may argue that this rule change has allowed offenses to be even more effective. Regardless of differing opinions, the reality is that receiving a serve with the hands is an option and clearly has made the game a bit less frustrating to learn for those who find it difficult to master the forearm pass.

To receive a serve with your hands, move your feet to the ball but keep the hands positioned above your shoulder height on contact. Contacting the ball below your shoulders could result in a held or lifted ball. Moving to the ball for this skill is just as important as forearm passing, and effective reaction to the serve and movement prior to contact will help you re-establish a solid athletic stance prior to contact. Your finger pads should contact the ball, and you should extend your arms toward the target.

The technical aspects and applications of setting and overhead passing will be covered in chapter 4, including the importance of the finger pads as contact points on the ball.

Talk, Talk, Talk

It is impossible to overemphasize the importance of systematic communication in the game of volleyball. During the reception of service, players should get in the habit of first calling the ball in or out, and then an individual should take charge by calling for the ball. Team communication can be as simple as "play" or "out." The chorus of shouts from teammates indicates that all the players are anticipating the serve and making a quick judgment as to whether the serve will be in. Obviously, the stronger the serve, the less time available for this call. It makes sense to keep all communication signals on court to short, one-syllable sounds if possible. Individual players who intend to pass the ball either from a serve or during a rally should simply call "ball" or "mine." What if two players call for the ball? Once again, a combination of nonverbal communication and perhaps a quick succession of "mine, MINE, **MINE**" is in order.

Your teammates not calling for the ball can be helpful with verbal cues ("you") and even nonverbal communication. Use body language to show a teammate in proximity that you are not taking the ball. If you are standing deep in the court with a strong serve sailing out of bounds, respond to teammates shouting "out" or "long" and just open up your stance, the way a matador does when the bull rushes by, and allow the ball to sail out of bounds.

Remember, it's a congested area shared by six teammates, so communication is the key!

TRIAD PASSING

In triad passing (figure 3.3), use progressions as needed to get players to work on passing in a game-like situation. Divide players into teams of three. Each group of three needs two balls (figure 3.3*a*). On each team, one player is the tosser, one is the target, and one is the passer. The tosser and target both have a ball. The tosser and passer line up behind opposite attack lines, and the target lines up near the net on the passer's side. The drill begins when the tosser tosses the ball to the passer, simulating a serve. The target immediately bounces her ball to the tosser. The passer calls for the ball from the tosser and passes it to the target. Once the target has this ball, the tosser again tosses to the passer. When the passer has successfully completed 10 passes to the target, the players switch roles.

Once players have had some opportunities to work on passing contacts, each group of three removes a ball, and the tosser becomes a server, who, based on ability level, can be directed to move continuously deeper in their own court to initiate the serve across the net (figure 3.3*b*).

To create a game-like scenario that continues to place emphasis on passing contacts, the target moves back and forth under the net each time the ball crosses the net and becomes the second touch by setting the first contacted ball back to that passer, who then delivers a forearm pass over the net. The sequence is repeated until an error occurs (figure 3.3*c*).

BUTTERFLY SERVING AND PASSING

In butterfly serving and passing (figure 3.4), you will learn to read and react to live serves by passing to the target. This is a full-court serving and passing drill. On each side is a team composed of two passers (one on the court and one or more waiting outside the sideline), one target near the net, and two or more servers (one to serve and one or more waiting to serve). The server serves to the passer on the opponent's side of the court, then runs to the other side to join the passing line. The passer passes to the target on his side of the court, then moves up to become the next target. The target catches the pass, then moves to the serving line. This is a continuous cycle: server to passer, passer to target, target to server. The only time a player changes sides of the court is after serving.

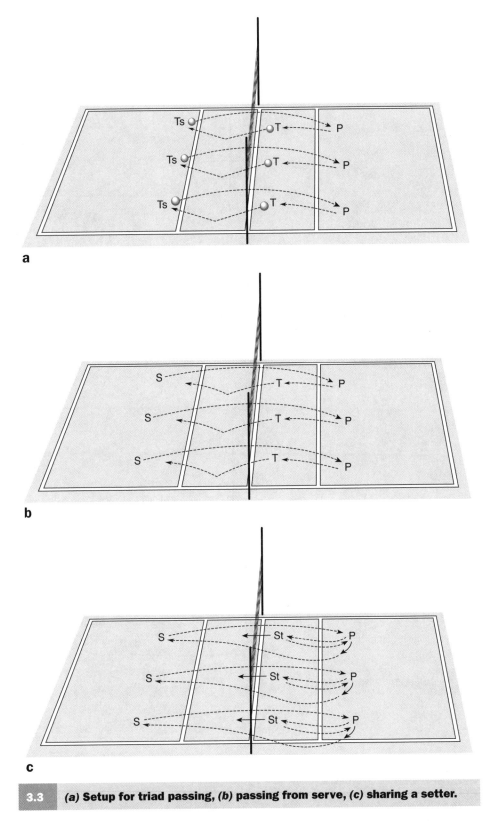

By adding a passer to each side of the court and creating a seam (figure 3.5), you can work on verbal ("mine" or "ball") and nonverbal communication with a teammate.

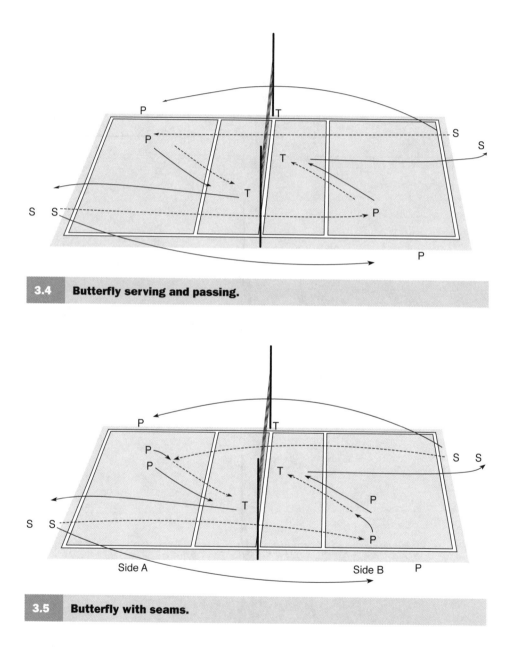

3.4 Butterfly serving and passing.

3.5 Butterfly with seams.

Setting

When asked to describe the necessary traits of a setter, coaches are likely to offer a variety of responses, including golden hands, nerves of steel, thick skin, leader of the pack, team quarterback, or better yet, a coach on the floor. They will also tell you that setters must develop and possess great vision, reaction, and instantaneous decision-making skills. You will discover that all of these are important as you gain a greater understanding of the complexities of attacking options within a team's offensive system (see chapter 11).

Although it is most common to have a designated player perform the role of setter, it is important to recognize that all players will find themselves in circumstances where they need to use their hands. As mentioned in chapter 3, setting, or overhead passing, as it is commonly referred to, can be used as a team's first touch to receive serve or free balls from an opponent. (We'll discuss this topic in more detail later in this chapter).

Let's start with the premise that at the moment of serve, one player on the receiving team has been predetermined and designated within an offensive system to receive the first team contact from a teammate and deliver it to an attacker. If you are the designated setter, you first need to move, if necessary, to the agreed-upon target area for your team's service reception. Let's split the net into nine zones, numbering them from left to right (figure 4.1). You want to establish

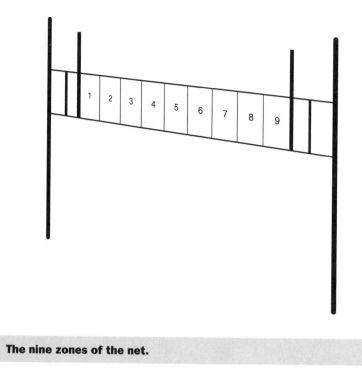

your position as a target for the passers in zone 6, just to the right of the center of the net. You should arrive at the target with your right shoulder near the net, but you should be ready to chase down an inaccurate serve receive contact.

Your communication as the designated setter is crucial. You have a few key responsibilities in terms of effective communication. First, provide a visible target for passers (right hand in the air) and then add a verbal signal ("here").

You will soon realize that a good percentage of passes will not arrive at the target.

The execution of most volleyball skills requires effective movement of players prior to contacting the ball. This is certainly true of setting. You must react to the pass and decide immediately if you can get to the ball and execute a set. If you decide to travel to the ball, the next key communication skill is to say "mine" as you move. Teammates need to give way when you call "mine" since you are claiming responsibility to get to the ball.

Coaches will train designated setters to move quickly and assertively in all directions to chase down a less than perfect first contact and to make the next play on the ball whenever possible. Your ultimate goal as the designated setter should be to get an available attacker a jump and a swing. If and when you determine that getting to the poor serve receive contact is not possible, you need to call for help. In this scenario, teammates need to be ready to step in and use their hands to set the ball to available attackers. The bread and butter drill (figure 4.11) allows you to work on this exact scenario.

You can do it

Technical Setting Keys

Once the ball has been passed to the target either with the hands or the forearms, we can refer to the set as the second touch. Since the goal is to control the ball using only three contacts and ultimately smash the ball into the opponent's court, accuracy and consistency will obviously play an important role in setting.

When executing a set (let's use net zone 1 as your target), focus on moving your feet to the ball (figure 4.2a), and upon arrival, your hands go up quickly. When I work with a setter, this idea of feet first and then hands will be reinforced constantly with verbal reminders of "feet [pause] hands." To be able to square your shoulders to the target, arrive at the spot where the ball is heading before it gets there. It is preferable to have your right foot forward, especially if a serve reception forces you near the net.

Next, as shown in figure 4.2b, form your hands in the shape of the volleyball. It is critical to have your thumbs pointed at your eyes. Practice this without a volleyball and you will be able to picture the ball settling into your hands quite nicely. Your goal should be to contact the ball near forehead level.

As you contact the ball with your finger pads (figure 4.2c), be sure to extend with both your arms and legs in the direction of the intended set (figure 4.2d).

4.2 Executing a set: *(a)* feet to ball, *(b)* ball-shaped hands, *(c)* finger pad contact, *(d)* extend with arms and legs.

SPRING IN THE WRISTS

The action of the wrists is important in the execution of a set. With your hands open and in the shape of the volleyball, your wrists will naturally give a little as the ball contacts your finger pads. This can be described as the ball going to the hands. Think of your wrists as a spring and be sure that the ball doesn't stop in your hands (figure 4.3*a*). This would result in a held ball violation. Use the natural spring of your wrists (figure 4.3*b*) to assist in pushing the ball back out of your hands.

4.3 *(a)* **Wrist spring,** *(b)* **extension after contact.**

One of my favorite drills to share with new learners is the spring drill. I ask a player to hold the ball in both hands in the setting position with the ball just in front of their forehead. I tell the player I am going to try to push the ball right into their forehead and that they need to resist this force without holding onto the ball. I push hard for about two seconds, then suddenly pull my hands quickly away from the ball, and it springs right in the air. This force creates the type of tension available in the wrists for setting.

MAKING CONTACT

The most common setting errors involve the contact of the ball. A player may hold the ball in the hands too long and actually be whistled for a held ball infraction. I like to refer to this as the "Hhrruuummmphhh" set.

You may have heard the phrase *deep dish*. That phrase adequately describes a setter who holds the ball before releasing it. The player receives the ball with hands near the forehead or face, holds the ball as it drops to chest level, then throws it into the air. To avoid the deep dish, think of your hands going to the ball as opposed to the ball going to your hands.

Another common setting mistake is the slapping sound resulting from a set that only contacts the palms of the hand and not the finger pads. The adjustment needed here is simply to focus on contacting the ball with the pads of the fingers. Jabbing or stabbing at the ball is even worse and most commonly is observed as a "hot potato"–type contact. Each of these errors requires focused practice opportunities on developing a softer touch on the ball.

THE BACK SET

As a setter, you are not always limited to setting to teammates in front of you. You can also send the ball to eligible attackers behind you with a back set. While the back set may be challenging for new players, the technical keys presented above in regard to body, arm, and hand position also relate in the execution of the back set.

Take another look at figure 4.1, and imagine yourself as the setter near net zone 6. A teammate has just passed the ball to you, your hands go up in the shape of the ball, and you decide to set to a teammate who will attack in net zone 9. You need to contact the ball near your forehead, but then as you slightly arch your back and drive with your arms, push the ball high to your target behind you (figure 4.4). This full extension should finish with your biceps near your ears. With experience and practice, you will gain confidence in setting to a player that you cannot see.

It is quite common for new players learning to back set to significantly arch their backs before contacting the ball as a way of helping get the set to a teammate behind them. When I train new setters, I use the setter neutral drill (figure 4.12) to help them keep a neutral body position prior to contact. As your game progresses, and if you become a designated setter, you will discover it is advantageous for your offense when the opposing blockers and defenders can't predict who you are going to set to based on your pre-contact body position.

4.4 **Back set.**

JUMP SETTING

As setters gain confidence and develop solid and consistent contact, jump setting can take an offense to the next level (see figure 4.5). Begin by recognizing that driving off the floor with the legs as part of the full extension described earlier is no longer available with a jump set. Now all the strength needed for the contact and finish will be provided by the upper body. Your execution of the jump set starts with all of the same pre-contact reaction and movement details already presented, but now your hands get to the passed ball faster because you are intercepting the ball sooner than if you remained on the ground. You must use your arms as you jump, which will naturally allow you to get your hands in the shape of the ball just prior to contact. With practice, you will develop the fine-tuning skills needed to make adjustments at contact to deliver sets of different heights to a variety of locations, as you will see later in this chapter (figure 4.7).

4.5 *(a)* **Jump to intercept ball,** *(b)* **contact at height of jump,** *(c)* **finish with arm extension.**

Jump setting can speed up a team's offensive tempo and create a number of advantages for a team. Teams with a left-handed player designated as a front-row setter create a real dilemma for blockers. Lefty setters with their right shoulder near the net are in position when they jump to turn and swing on the second contact since they are an eligible attacker (figure 4.6).

4.6   **Turn and swing (option for lefty).**

OVERHEAD PASSING

As introduced in chapter 3, the rules of volleyball allow a double contact on any first team contact, including the use of the hands. The average observer of the sport, who is unfamiliar with the rules, will often wonder why the official allows these double hits to go un-whistled while the next touch by a setter with a clear double contact is whistled. The only judgment call allowed by officials on a first team contact is a held ball. Players receiving the serve with their hands need to keep that in mind and be sure to keep their hands moving toward the ball throughout contact.

Receiving the serve with the hands can be useful on short serves or on high float serves that don't travel with a lot of force. Remember, the force of a jump serve could be so great that the ball comes to rest in the receiver's hands before it can be pushed out. With experience, you can anticipate, react to the type of serve, and choose whether to use the forearm pass or overhead pass to receive the serve and direct the ball to the setter.

A second common use of the overhead pass occurs when the designated setter decides it's not possible to get to the first touch and shouts for help. The teammate nearest the errant serve receive pass should respond to the setter's help signal by stepping in and attempting to set the ball to a teammate near one of the antennae. This is the essential play for a teammate to execute when helping a setter. The primary goal is to get an attacker able to jump and swing on this play. All teammates must understand their responsibilities when the setter calls "help" (see figure 4.11).

Finally, when the opponent gives an easy free ball over the net, this is another time to contact the ball with an overhead pass if possible. Precise and accurate contacts on a free ball are critical for success. (See chapter 10 for more detail.) Most coaches favor the use of the hands whenever their team receives a free ball. The five-person setting drill in figure 4.10 is a practice opportunity for using the hands in several situations during a rally.

Take it to the court

Be a Designated Setter

The setter needs some additional help with setting up a communication system so as to identify to teammates in advance where and how high the ball will be set. If we use the zones of the net to establish the location of the set, then we need to add a numbering system to establish the height of the set.

In figure 4.7, the three sample sets are labeled with a two-digit number. The first number identifies the location of the set along the net. The second number indicates the approximate height (in feet). The 14 set would travel to zone 1 and would be set approximately four to six feet above the height of the net. The 51 set would travel to zone 5 but would be only one to two feet above the net. A 92 set is a back set that would travel to zone 9 with a height of two to four feet above the net.

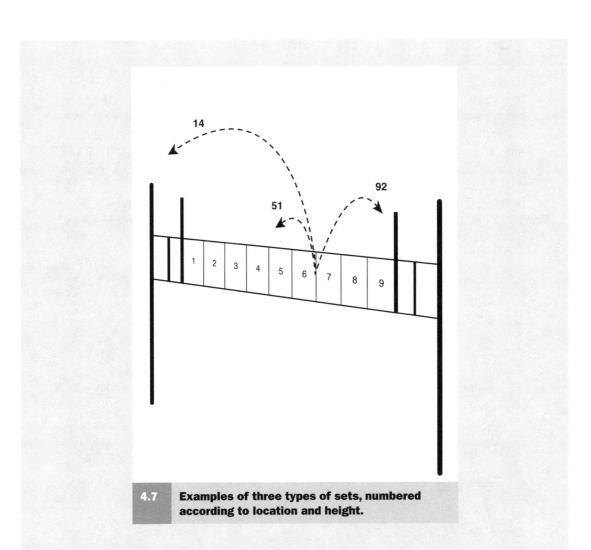

4.7 Examples of three types of sets, numbered according to location and height.

As you move into chapter 5 (Attacking), you will discover how the height of these sets relates to timing and tempo.

Give it a go

TRIADS AND BUTTERFLY DRILLS

The forearm passing drills in chapter 3 (figures 3.3 and 3.4) provide a great place to start to work on the overhead pass. Simply change the focus by replacing forearm passes with overhead passes.

THREE-PERSON SETTING

In the three-person setting drill (figure 4.8), you will learn to control the distance of sets and practice back sets. Four groups of three players work together, beginning about 15 feet (5 m) apart. Player A on one sideline faces player B in the middle. Player C on the other sideline and player B both face player A. Player A tosses the ball up in the air above the head and sets the ball to player B with a front set. Player B attempts a back set to player C, who pushes the ball high in the air back to player A. The cycle is repeated 10 times. After 10 cycles, the players rotate positions. Repeat until each player has had two turns at each position.

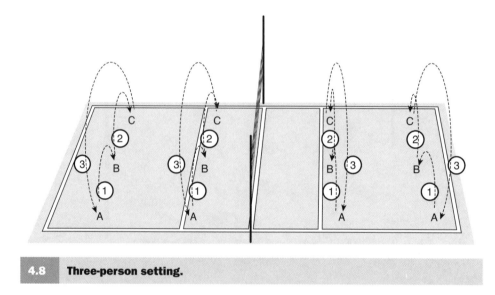

4.8 Three-person setting.

SETTING 14S

In this drill, you will practice setting 14 sets (see figure 4.7) from court zone 2 and net zone 6. A total of six players begin in one of three lines (figure 4.9), using both sides of the net. The tosser begins in court zone 5 with a ball in hand. The setter begins in court zone 2 and net zone 6. The attacker begins in court zone 4 and net zone 1. One player begins in line behind the tosser, setter, and attacker. Each player in the tossing line begins with a ball. The tosser tosses the ball to the setter, simulating a pass from a serve, and then follows the ball to the end of the setter's line. The setter sets the ball to the attacker with a 14 set, then moves to the end of the attacker's line.

The attacker catches the set and moves to the end of the tosser's line. This drill could be timed or continued until each player has a certain number of setting opportunities.

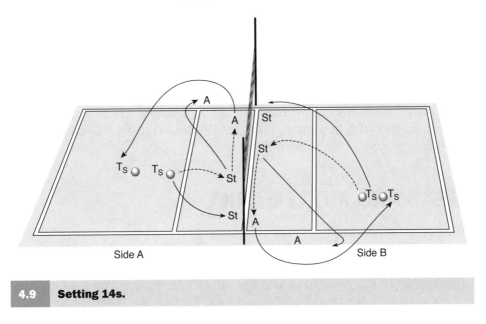

Side A   Side B

4.9   **Setting 14s.**

FIVE-PERSON SETTING DRILL

The five-person setting drill (figure 4.10) works the overhead pass in a variety of ways. Five players work together in this drill. Player A stands near court zone 5 with a ball and begins the drill by tossing

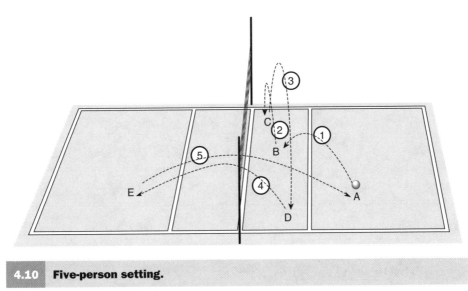

4.10   **Five-person setting.**

the ball in the air and setting to player B, who is near net zone 6. The set from player A simulates an overhead pass to set a free ball to the setter. Player B gives a 92 back set (see figure 4.7) to player C, who is near net zone 9. Player C sets a 14 to player D, who is 5 to 10 feet (2 to 3 m) away from net zone 1. Player D takes the ball that is away from the net and sends it across the net to player E, simulating the option of giving a free ball to the opponent with an overhead pass. Player E sets the ball back to player A to simulate a free ball given to the opponent. This cycle is repeated five times, then each player rotates to the position of the player they were setting to. The drill continues until each player has had two opportunities in each position.

BREAD AND BUTTER DRILL

This drill is fundamental to developing consistent setting skills. You will practice assisting a setter who calls for help on a service reception that is far away from the target. Twelve players form two lines: a line of setters (St) and a line of attackers (A). The instructor/ coach stands near the net with a basket of volleyballs (figure 4.11) and tosses (or bounces) a ball high in the air near the middle of the court to simulate a poor service reception that would result in the designated setter having to call for help. The first player in the setting line calls "mine," while the first player in the attacking zone

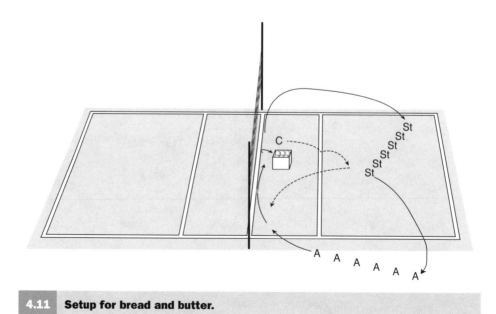

4.11   Setup for bread and butter.

calls for a 14. The ball is set toward the antenna, and the attacker runs, jumps, and catches the ball with two hands high and in front of him. That player drops the ball in the basket and moves to the end of the setting line, while the setter executes the set and moves to the end of the attacking line.

Once you've mastered the basic bread and butter drill, try this variation. After three minutes, the two lines switch responsibilities. The setting line now attempts to set the ball high in the air for a 94 set.

SETTER NEUTRAL

This drill is designed to assist you in keeping your body (especially upper body) in the same pre-contact position prior to setting a front or back set. A line of two or three setters begins in zone 1 of the court. Players in net zones 1 and 9 will be the targets and catch the sets (figure 4.12). The setters have been instructed to set a 14 or 94 based on command. The coach who has a ball in hand says "go," and the first setter moves toward net zone 6. Just as they arrive, the ball is tossed high in the air to the setter, and when it reaches the highest point, the coach shouts either "14" or "94." The setter attempts to respond by following the command. The target catches the ball and bounces it back to the coach. The setter returns to the end of the setting line as the next setter takes a turn. To challenge the setter, the 14 or 94 command can be given a moment or two after the ball reaches its height and is descending to the setter.

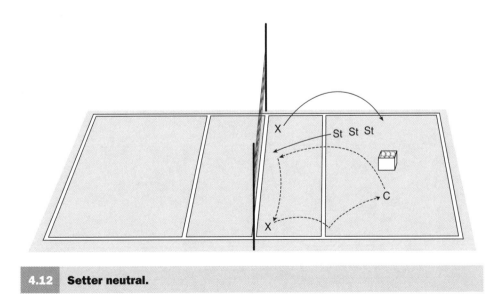

4.12   **Setter neutral.**

Attacking

Run, jump, and swing. If you want to learn to attack, you need to combine these three keys. If the setter's job is to get a jump and swing for an attacker on each play, then the attacker's job is to be available and ready to get that job done. Attackers need to anticipate and react to the set, effectively use a series of steps, get airborne, then use one of their attack options to score. We have discussed the first and second touch options; now we will look at that third and final touch.

At the highest levels of volleyball, the offense appears to have clear advantage over the defense, partly because of the athletic ability of elite athletes and partly because of the myriad attack options that can be used to put the block and defense at a disadvantage. Anyone who has watched experienced players has probably been wowed by a spectacular spike. We need to take it one step at a time, so we will begin with the footwork sequence.

The Attack

As you practice the run phase of the attack, approach the net at a 45-degree angle. If you are left-handed, begin by attacking from court zone 2. If you are right-handed, begin in court zone 3 or 4. Refer back to the "Righties and Lefties" section of chapter 1 for a reminder of why this is important.

Prior to your approach, your arms should hang naturally at your sides. Begin your approach behind the attack line. Drive forward and finish with a three-step sequence. For right-handed players, the first of the three steps (often called the timing step) needs to be with the left foot as your arms swing forward naturally. As shown in figure 5.1*a*, the attack line is a great reference point for this step.

The second step is a running step on the right foot, often called a directional step (figure 5.1*b*). The directional step allows you to adjust to the set and in most cases brings you near the net. Drive your arms back as you accelerate toward the net.

The final step with the left foot brings you back into balance so you can jump off two feet to attack (figure 5.1*c*). Jumping off two feet allows you to transfer forward momentum from the run to a controlled vertical leap. On those last two steps, incorporate a heel-toe strike with your feet. This will result in a type of braking action and prevent net violations.

Many accomplished players may recall days and weeks of hearing "left [pause] right, left" from a coach as a helpful reminder of the correct sequence and related tempo of the final three steps in the approach. (Lefties would hear, "right [pause] left, right.") Think of it this way: during your approach, move from slow to fast and from low to high. You may eventually use four (or more) steps as part of the approach, but the final three steps need to follow the sequence outlined above.

Use both arms to jump. As you move into the two quick closing steps, your arms should swing back and then drive up into the air as you jump. Once airborne, you want to get to the high draw (sometimes called bow and arrow) position. Reach high and use your extended non-attacking arm to sight the ball as you draw your attacking elbow back.

The attacking swing requires a whip-like action of the arm, keeping the elbow above the shoulder throughout the swing, finishing with a full reach for the ball. Contact the ball with an open hand, high and in back of the ball to create topspin (figure 5.1*d*). Keeping the ball in front of your attacking shoulder and contacting the ball

5.1 *(a)* **Run (timing step),** *(b)* **run (directional step),** *(c)* **jump off two feet,** *(d)* **swing.**

with an open hand in the shape of the ball will assist you in creating topspin (forward spin). You will discover that your hand position on the ball also will help you avoid or hit around the block. Wrapping your hand around the inside of the ball with your thumb down will assist in hitting angle or crosscourt shots. Wrap your hand around the outside of the ball with the thumb up to hit cut-back shots. The whip-like action of the arm requires a full follow-through.

You may encounter some challenges with mastering the attack, but now you have plenty to work on. The fundamentals for attacking are indeed fun to practice. You will see steady improvement if you master the step sequence. You have a lot of court to work with, so don't try to pound the ball straight down. Hit the ball with topspin deep into the opponent's court. Make your opponent try to control the ball and counterattack.

More to choose and use

OFF-SPEED ATTACKS

Depending on the effectiveness of the block, an off-speed attack may be a good option. The tip (figure 5.2) is a deceptive attack disguised by a strong approach and dynamic jump. Instead of swinging at the ball, reach high with a locked elbow, contacting the ball with your finger pads. Place the ball just over the blockers' hands and on the floor in open space not covered by defenders.

5.2 The tip.

Another common off-speed shot is the roll shot (figure 5.3). Again, disguise this attack by completing a strong, aggressive approach. Near the height of your jump, as your arm comes forward, use a small circular motion and roll or chip the ball with an off-speed topspin motion. Tactically, the roll shot is similar to the tip in that you are hoping to get defenders on their heels expecting a strong swing as you carefully place the ball over the block and on the floor in front of the defenders caught off guard.

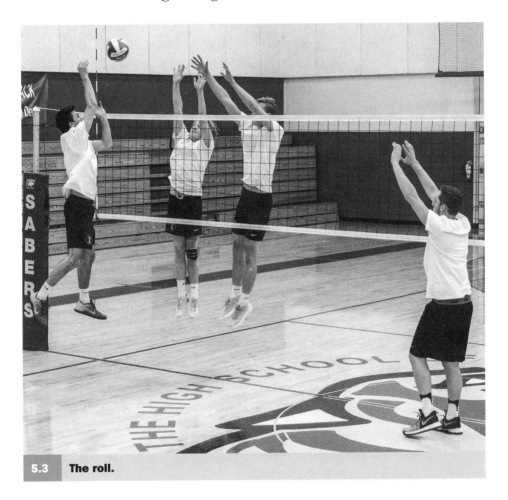

5.3 **The roll.**

SCORING OFF THE BLOCK

Accomplished players learn that in some cases the block is the attacker's best friend. They simply beat the ball off the blocker nearest the sideline and in fact aim for that blocker's outside hand. This is referred to as "tooling the block" (figure 5.4). We use tools in the workshop, thus using the block to score is considered a tool.

5.4 Tooling the block.

BACK-ROW ATTACK

Players who are legally positioned in the back row can also get in the act as long as they stay within the rules and jump with both feet behind the attack line to attack a ball that is above the height of the net. Back-row players approach the attack line with the same footwork sequence as outlined earlier. Keep in mind that often a player in the back row may first receive the serve and then will need to quickly move deep enough in the court to allow for a full approach. Back-row attackers can simply use "A," "B" (or "pipe"), and "C" as

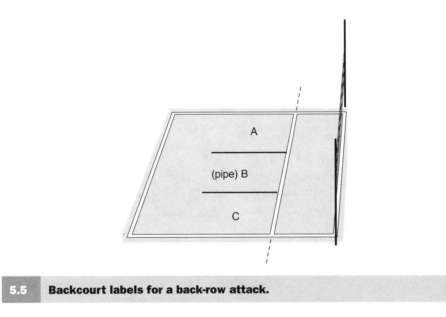

the verbal signals for attacks in court zones 5, 6, and 1, respectively (figure 5.5). You will be able to practice this situation using the two-tempo drill later in this chapter.

HITTING A DOWN BALL

Since we do not want to give our opponent an easy free ball, we need to consider what we can do with a third team contact when we cannot attack (e.g., if you approach the net to attack but the set ends up several feet behind you). You can't jump and swing but could adjust your footwork and step back, keeping the ball in front of you and attacking it while standing on the floor (figure 5.6). This is called a down ball. Think of it as hitting a topspin serve from the court instead of the service area. With practice, players can effectively give the opponent a tough third contact even when they can't jump and swing.

If you are not able to jump and swing at a set, you need to move behind the ball quickly. As the ball approaches, step forward with your nondominant foot, raise both arms, and get your upper body into the high draw position.

If you are right-handed, get your left foot forward and left hand up and then whip your right arm to the ball, reaching high and using an open hand to create topspin. Remember, you'll have a little more court to work with if you attack deep to a corner of the opponent's court rather than down the line. A down ball (an attack from the

Hitting a down ball.

floor) often will be much more difficult for your opponent to handle than a free ball. The goal is to never give an easy free ball; replace it with a down ball whenever possible.

One other strategy to consider when you need to give your opponent a free ball is to try to make the designated setter take the first touch. Keep aware of where the opponent's designated setter is playing on defense.

THE SLIDE: USING THE ONE-FOOT TAKEOFF

With all this talk about going off two feet, you may be wondering about the explosive attack with a one-foot takeoff you have likely seen used by elite players. If a player can take a running approach along the net instead of at the net, a one-foot takeoff can be very effective (figure 5.7a). This attack is referred to as the slide and is most commonly used by a designated middle attacker who travels behind the setter and chases a back set heading toward the antennae. If attackers in court zone 3 wanted to hit a 92 with a slide, they could run past the setter and use the same footwork used for a basketball layup. Use the antenna as the imaginary hoop. When the ball arrives there, take a swing at it. Often your momentum will carry you out of bounds, so quickly recover and get back on the court, ready to play.

For a right-handed middle attacker, move behind the setter and drive the right knee up as you jump off the left foot. At the same time, both arms need to go up to allow for a smooth and natural arm swing to complete this dynamic attack option (figure 5.7b). Offensive systems of play (see chapter 11) could also incorporate a slide for you as a lefty, wherein you would most often be traveling from a starting point behind the setter and chasing a front set that pushes you toward the left antennae.

5.7 *(a)* The one-foot takeoff or slide, *(b)* slide arm swing.

It's All in the Timing

Perhaps the toughest part of attacking is the timing involved with different sets. Let's take a look at tempo and timing.

By referring back to the zones of the net and heights of sets (figure 4.7), we can establish some basic ground rules. Students of the game often ask, "When do I leave for the attack?" That is a good question. A rule of thumb for high outside sets such as the 14 is to take all your steps after the ball is set. That keeps it simple. If that is true, then for a set like a 51, you take all your steps before the ball is set. That will be simple for the attacker but not so easy for the setter since the quick set is a more advanced skill. Deductive reasoning should help you determine when to leave for a set like a 92. Some steps need to be taken before the ball is set and some steps after it is set.

Volleyball coaches refer to these three tempos as quick or first tempo (51), second tempo (92), and third tempo (14). Two of the attacking drills—the all-the-steps-before drill and the all-the-steps-after drill—will help you work on timing and tempo for attacks.

These tempos are not limited to front-row attacks. Watch elite teams play and you may see a back-row player hitting a first-tempo set (just high enough for the jumping player to reach). This back-row "quick" is often called a "bic."

MASTERING THE APPROACH

The run phase of the attack is vital to successful attacking. This drill reinforces proper technique for the run phase. Six players begin on the attack lines of a court (figure 5.8). Righties start in court zones 3 or 4; lefties use court zone 2. All players take a full approach and simulate the arm swing on each approach. Players execute five approaches for each of the seven points of emphasis listed below, focusing on the parts of the attack one at a time:

1. Approach the net at a 45-degree angle.
2. Focus on "left [pause] right, left" or "right [pause] left, right."
3. Use a natural arm swing.
4. Concentrate on the heel-toe braking action.

5. Jump off two feet.

6. Jump with both arms in the air.

7. Use a whip-like action of the attack arm.

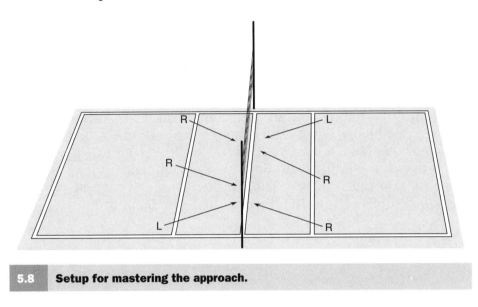

5.8 Setup for mastering the approach.

ALL THE STEPS BEFORE

Let's work on a first-tempo attack in which all the steps are taken before the ball is set. Six attackers begin at the attack line in court zone 3 (figure 5.9). The coach/instructor has a ball in hand and a basket of balls nearby. An attacker takes an approach and swings the

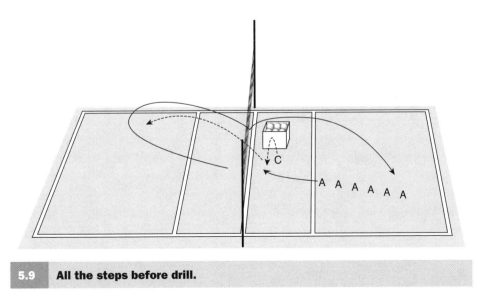

5.9 All the steps before drill.

arm for a 51 set. The coach tosses the ball directly to the attacker's hand for the attack. All of the attacker's steps occur before the ball is tossed to simulate the timing of a quick or first-tempo attack. The attacker chases the attack, retrieves the ball, and places it in the basket, then gets back in line.

ALL THE STEPS AFTER

Now we will move into a third-tempo attack in which all steps are taken after the ball is set. Six attackers begin at the attack line in court zone 4 (figure 5.10). The coach/instructor has a ball in hand and a basket of balls nearby. The attacker leaves to attack once the coach tosses the ball to simulate a 14 set. All the attacker's steps occur after the ball is tossed. The attacker chases the attack, retrieves the ball and places it in the basket, then gets back in line.

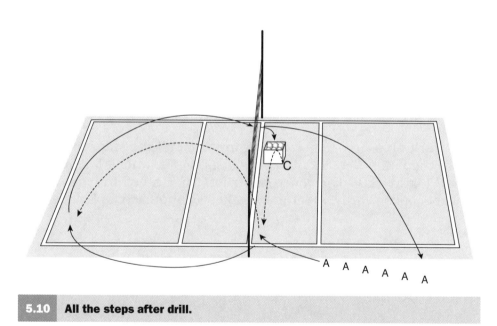

5.10 **All the steps after drill.**

PASS, SET, HIT

Here's your chance to practice passing, hitting, and setting—all the skills you've learned so far. Twelve players join one of three lines (figure 5.11). On one side of the net, four players are in a setting line in court zone 2 and four players are in a passing line in court zone 5. On the other side of the net, four players each have a ball and are in a line in court zone 1. The tosser tosses across the net to the passer and moves to the end of the setting line. The passer passes the ball to the setter, calls for a 14, and approaches to attack. The setter delivers a 14 and goes to the end of the passing line. The passer completes the drill by attacking the ball, chasing and retrieving it, and going to the tossing line. This drill continues for a timed period or until each player has had 20 attempts to pass and swing. You may also try this variation: serve to initiate rather than toss, and direct the server to defend in court zone 5 to create a target for the attacker.

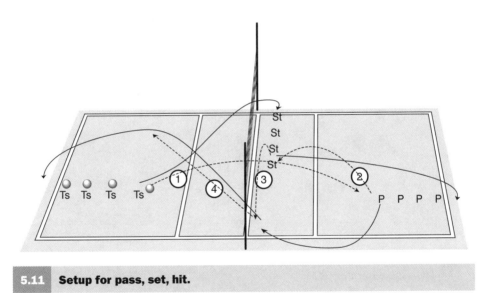

5.11 **Setup for pass, set, hit.**

TWO-TEMPO DRILL

Here is a game-like drill that teaches you to execute a first or third tempo, based on who handles the serve. As shown in figure 5.12, one setter and two passers start on the court on side B, with another pair of passers ready to rotate on the court. Three blockers are in position on side A, where a server initiates each rally and then takes a back-row position on the court. The rules for the passers are as follows: (1) If you pass the ball, you then attack (third tempo) from the back row by calling for an A, B, or C. (2) The non-passer must approach for a 51 (first tempo). The drill allows the passer and attackers to work on timing based on the height and location of the serve receive and to practice making themselves available for two different tempos based on which passer receives serve. When the side A blockers and defenders are able to keep the play alive, rallies continue until one side wins the point. Passers remain on the court for five serves or a game to five points, and then two new passers enter the court. All court positions can be rotated periodically.

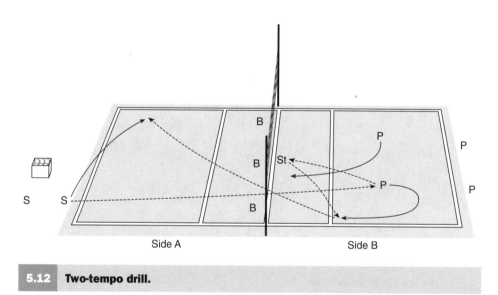

5.12 Two-tempo drill.

Blocking

Domination of an opponent in volleyball is most likely to result from either service aces or uncontested attacks. Attackers are on the offensive: they know in advance the height and location of the set and are poised to drive the ball to the floor. The first line of defense against this attack is the block. Blockers have several basic responsibilities. The first priority is to avoid giving up uncontested attacks. The front-row defenders need to identify which attacker they have primary responsibility for, stay in front of that attacker as they approach the net, and get their hands over the net in front of the attacker's arm. Think of these duties in three parts: see the hitter, front the hitter, and seal the net.

A second priority is for a blocker or a group of blockers working together to put up a wall of hands in front of an attacker. Blockers always hope to intercept the attack with their hands, but it is equally important for team defense that the individual or collective block takes a portion of the court away from the attacker based on their positioning. If the block can channel the attack to portions of the court, then the team can place defenders in those areas. We will build on these concepts in chapter 9, Team Defense. For now, let's start by getting the block in front of the hitters.

The Block

As a front-row defender, you need to be within an arm's length of the net at the moment your teammate serves the ball. Stand in a ready position with your hands above shoulder level, knees slightly bent, and toes pointed directly at the centerline (figure 6.1*a*). Keep in mind that your opponent has three basic front-row attack options—left, middle, and right. You and your front-row blocking teammates need to identify these players and assume primary responsibility for the adjacent attacker. Additionally, it is essential to identify the opponent's designated setter and determine if that player is a front-row player (eligible to jump and swing) or a back-row player. Blockers must be ready to block setters, especially lefties, as we saw in figure 4.6, when they decide to attack instead of setting to a teammate.

To execute a block from the ready position, simply bend your knees (think of this as a coil), keeping your hands open and in the same position above your shoulders; use elbow drive as you explode into the air (figures 6.1*b* and 6.1*c*). Your goal is to get both hands across the plane of the net and then make a controlled, cushioned landing by keeping your knees bent (figure 6.1*d*).

As the attacker approaches the net, the blocker should attempt to use side shuffle steps to stay in front of the hitter. Any movement should end with the blocker back in the balanced ready position, prepared to jump off both feet. The blocker's cardinal rule for timing is to jump only after the attacker jumps.

The blocker should penetrate the plane of the net by leading with the heels of the hands. Blockers should keep their thumbs close to each other, allowing their hands to work as a unit and surround the ball. When the hands are across the net, have them face zone 6 of the opponent's court to avoid being tooled by the attacker. Your blocking skill may make the difference between winning or losing, between grabbing or sustaining the momentum for your team or giving up the momentum to your opponents.

6.1 *(a)* Ready, hands shoulder height, *(b)* coil, *(c)* explode and seal the net, *(d)* cushion the landing.

Learn the skills and techniques of blocking and practice them. Your team will be better for it.

WATCHING FOR CUES

What does the blocker watch throughout the blocking sequence? At first glance, you might think blockers simply need to watch the ball, ending up with their hands in front of the ball. Although that will often work, a more effective strategy is to begin watching the ball as soon as it is contacted by the receiving team. Remember, the pass may come right over the net.

If the ball is passed to the setter, focus on the ball in the setter's hands since the setter has the option of sending it over the net. Once the setter sends the ball to an attacker, watch the ball long enough to determine where it will end up, then focus on the attacker. The eye sequence for the blocker is to watch the ball as it is passed, watch the ball in the hands of the setter, watch the direction and height of the ball (after the setter has released it) just long enough to know where it will end up (then the blocker moves quickly to front the hitter), and lastly, watch the attacker. You can shorten these key ideas to "ball, setter, ball, hitter" to use as a reminder when blocking.

An additional advantage of watching the hitter just prior to the block is that the blocker is the first one to see the arm action of the attacker. This is especially important if the attacker chooses to use a tip or a roll shot.

GETTING THE HANDS OVER THE NET

A blocker's most common challenge involves getting the hands over the net. Blockers should always keep their hands in front of their face and head to avoid moving their arms and hands behind their head when jumping. This movement results in throwing the hands at and onto the net. Be sure that at any point in the block you can see the backs of your hands (figure 6.2). If you can't see the backs of your hands, they are in the wrong place. Another helpful hint is to keep the chin down as you jump and reach over the net. Throwing the head back will make it very difficult to seal the net with the hands.

It is perfectly legal to reach over the net to block. You just need to let the attacker have the first chance to touch the ball on her side of the net. The ideal block is one that results in the ball being contacted on the opponent's side of the net and going straight down on that side. Players refer to this as a *roof*. The angle of the arms reaching over the net should look like the angle of a roof on a house (figure 6.3). In most cases, even at the highest levels of the game, the blockers don't dominate at the net, so the position of the block is just as important, if not more so, than those rally-ending roofs.

6.2 Seal the net.

6.3 The roof.

USING THE SOFT BLOCK

What about players who cannot reach over the net? They can still be effective by establishing good position for a multiple block. Additionally, a vertically challenged player can use a soft block by positioning his hands a few inches from the net with wrists cocked back, similar to a setting position (figure 6.4). An attacked ball contacting strong blocking hands placed in this position will often rebound high into the air and to a backcourt defender on the blocker's team. This contact does not count as a team or individual contact for the indoor game, so it is an effective way to slow down the ball and keep it in play.

6.4 | Soft block.

Group Blocking

Although a blocker may need to execute a single block without help, multiple players may also work together to block. A group block is most common on a ball set to net zone 1 or zone 9, what we refer to as an outside set to a pin hitter or a set near the "pin" (antenna). The outside blocker (right front or left front player) is responsible for establishing the position of a multiple-player block by using quick shuffle steps to front the hitter. The mirror drill (figure 6.9) provides an ideal opportunity to work on this.

The middle blocker not only has primary responsibility for the opponent's middle attacker but also must watch for outside sets and attempt to join teammates to put up a wall of hands. This sideways movement will require more than short shuffle steps. Side-to-side movement of blockers requires short runs along the net, ending with a blocker in a balanced position, ready to jump with the outside blocker just after the attacker has left the ground. This can best be performed by using a step, crossover step, closing step pattern. To crossover step to the left, take a running step to the left with your left foot, cross your right foot in front of your left foot, then step to the left again with your left foot. To crossover step to the right, take a running step to the right with your right foot, cross your left foot in front of your right foot, then step to the right again with your right foot.

An outside blocker may also use crossover steps to travel more than a few feet to either side. A middle blocker can add a side shuffle step to the end of the crossover step pattern to make a small final adjustment to end up shoulder to shoulder with his teammate.

The middle blocker is responsible for closing the space between the two blockers and relies on the outside blocker to establish the position of the multiple block. The middle blocker's outside foot should end up 4 to 6 inches (10-12 cm) from the inside foot of the outside blocker.

Both blockers keep their hands facing the opponent's court zone 6, especially the outside blocker (see figure 6.5). Remember, the attacker could be looking to tool the block, and the outside hand of the outside blocker is an inviting target.

6.5 **Blocking hands face the opponent's zone 6.**

Swing Blocking

A second technical approach to blocking is swing blocking. Figure 6.6 illustrates the dynamic and synchronized movements of teammates turning and essentially running along the net in the direction of the opponent's set and swinging the arms to help elevate them to challenge the attacker. Competitive players in a team setting would need ample time to perfect the movements and the timing of the sweeping motion of the arms while their body squares back up and hands reach across the net to defend the attack.

One of my coaches used to say that team sports require athletes to go directly from one job to the next, and this is true for the blocker. Blockers need to be prepared to keep playing after executing a block. Many attacks end up going past or over the block, and the blocker should try to watch the ball even as it goes past. If the head follows the eyes, and if the body follows the head, then the blocker would naturally turn toward backcourt teammates when landing, just in case a ball is dug and comes right back at the blocker. The block and turn drill (figure 6.10) trains a player for this situation.

Finally, a word about communication. Prior to the serve, each blocker should signal to his teammates the uniform numbers of the opposing front-row players who are eligible attackers. Outside blockers can also give a "right here" cue to the middle blocker once they have made their final adjustment steps to get in front of a hitter. This helps the middle blocker when following the "ball, setter, ball, hitter" eye sequence. The middle blocker may have time to peek at the outside blocker, but hearing the outside blocker is helpful. When the middle blocker arrives with the outside blocker before the attacker leaves the ground, the outside blocker can give the timing cue "ready, go" to make sure both players jump at the same time.

A beach or grass court blocker playing in a two-on-two match often signals the server with one or two fingers behind the back prior to service. One finger indicates "I'm blocking line"; two fingers means "I'm blocking angle." Indoor players may have a scouting report on preferred attack tendencies of opposing hitters and could easily use this system as well.

6.6 Swing block sequence: *(a)* turn and run, *(b)* jump with arm swing, *(c)* hands seal the net.

ON THE FLOOR BLOCKING

When you block, you need to surround the ball with your hands. For this drill, 12 players work in pairs using any available court space. Stand on the floor across from your partner, reaching high and in front of your body with your hands in the blocking position (figure 6.7). Your partner holds a volleyball with the nondominant hand within six inches of your hands and from a high draw arm position attacks the ball with the dominant hand into the block. Both of you stay on the floor throughout the drill. As the blocker, you should attempt to surround the attacked ball with your hands and keep your eyes on the ball.

6.7 **On the floor blocking.**

BALL EXCHANGE

It's important to practice reaching over the net. For the ball exchange drill, eight players form pairs and stand across the net from each other. You should attempt to match up with a player who is similar in size and jumping ability. One player starts with the ball in both hands and jumps, raising the ball above the height of the net, and the other should reach over the net to take the ball out of the jumper's hands (figure 6.8). This action will simulate the blocking action of reaching over the net. Each pair needs to exchange the ball back and forth over the net 10 times in a row.

6.8 Ball exchange.

MIRROR DRILL

In the mirror drill (figure 6.9), you will practice fronting the hitter. Six players work in pairs at the net. Three players begin on the attack line, each with a blocker across the net in front of them in a ready position. Each attacker needs to take a quick approach to either side of the blocker. The attacker approaches and takes a simulated swing. The blocker reacts to the movement of the attacker and uses side shuffle steps to get in front of the hitter and jump to block just after the attacker leaves the ground. Each attacker must approach 10 times; then the attackers switch positions and roles with their partner.

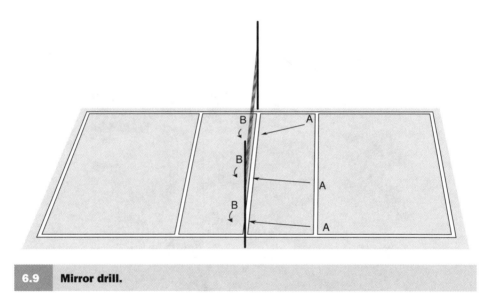

6.9 Mirror drill.

SIDE-TO-SIDE SHUFFLE

Effective blocking requires that you move. In this drill, you will practice using side shuffle steps to the left and right. Eight blockers form two lines in court zone 4 on each side of the net. The first player in each line assumes the ready position for blocking and takes a side shuffle and close step to their right, followed by a block. This is repeated two more times as the player travels toward the other sideline and then moves to the back of the line opposite from where they started. The drill continues until each player has taken two complete trips on each side of the net. The drill can be extended by restarting with both lines in court zone 2; all players will then move to their left for two complete trips on each side of the net.

STEP, CROSSOVER STEP, AND CLOSE

This drill continues to work on movement, except middle blockers will practice the step, crossover step, and close pattern to the left and right. Eight blockers form two lines in court zone 4 on each side of the net. The first player in each line assumes the ready position for blocking and takes a step, crossover step, and close step to their right, followed by a block. This is repeated one more time as the player travels toward the other sideline and then moves to the back of the line opposite from where they started. Continue the drill until each player has taken two complete trips on each side of the net. The drill can be extended by restarting with both lines in court zone 2; all players will then move to their left for two complete trips on each side of the net.

BLOCK AND TURN

After attempting to block the ball, you need to turn and get ready for the next play.

In this drill the coach acts as a back-row setter who digs the attack, creating a scenario wherein the right front player needs to set the ball. Four players on side B form a line in court zone 4, each with a ball in hand and prepared to attack a 14 (figure 6.10). Two other players on side A form a blocking line near court zone 2. The first player in this line assumes the ready blocking position. Play is initiated when the first side B attacker tosses to a setter, who returns the ball with a 14. The attacker attempts to hit down the line where a player is positioned to collect the ball, place it in the basket, and move to the blocking line. Regardless of the result of the swing, the blocker turns toward the coach as soon as possible after the block, takes a toss from the coach, and sets a 14 to a target on side A. The side B attacker runs to side A to serve as the next ball collector, the blocker becomes the next target, and the target keeps the ball and moves to the end of side B attacking line. The drill continues for a timed period or until each player has performed a certain number of repetitions.

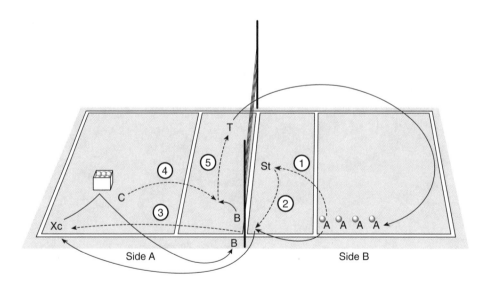

6.10 **Block and turn.**

Digging

Often when we watch volleyball we are thrilled by the diving, rolling saves that players make when they hit the floor. But that is not where we want to start. We need to begin by working on retrieving the attack that is hit right at us. If a team has to rely on fantastic and exciting saves made by players leaving their feet, they are in trouble. Yes, those great plays can turn around the momentum of a game, and they are critical, but the foundation of effective digging begins with defensive positioning and technique that allows players to stay on their feet, keep the ball off the floor, and better yet, control the ball on their own side of the net so the defense can transition to offense with a counterattack.

In any number of sports, a case can be made that defense is an attitude. After many coaching seasons, I grew fond of identifying any moment when the ball was about to land on our side of the net as a "personal emergency." As players adopted this mind-set, I had a front-row seat for some incredible plays; nothing brings volleyball fans out of their seats like a fantastic effort in a seemingly lost cause by players who somehow keep their team in the point. ESPN plays of the day in volleyball most commonly are great defensive plays made by players who do whatever it takes not to let the ball hit the floor.

One of the volleyball basics highlighted in chapter 1 was reading, which involves (1) carefully and intently observing an opponent about to send the ball over the net, and (2) anticipating, reacting, and effectively moving to make a play on that ball. In no other aspect of the game is reading needed more than digging or retrieving an attacked ball. Remember there is only one ball in play, and keeping it off the floor starts with reading and reacting.

The Dig

Stay low—two simple words to keep in mind when your opponent has the ball and you are not involved in the block. The attacked ball is going to go to the floor, so you need to be near the floor. There are two key moments to discuss: (1) the moment of attack and (2) your contact.

To be ready to dig, you need to be ready to move (figure 7.1*a*) and in a position to see the attacker's upper body. During the attacker's arm swing, you want to be low and have your shoulders forward in case you need to move forward for an off-speed attack. When I was learning to play the game competitively, I was taught to step-hop into this body position just prior to the attacker's contact. Over time as a coach, I picked up the phrase "split-step" to share with players to accomplish the same thing. At that moment, where you are preparing to react to the swing, your hands should be apart and away from your body, both in front of and outside your hips (figure 7.1*b*).

It is essential to keep your arms apart in the ready position so you will be prepared to dig a ball hit to either side of your body. If you put your arms together and move them as a unit, your contact with the ball will likely result in the ball flying off the court in the direction your arms were moving.

The key idea to remember when digging is to absorb. The attack often has some heat on it. The attacker will be trying to use topspin and put the ball on the floor. Your goal is to put or keep your body behind the attacked ball. Your hands and arms will form a platform similar to what you have practiced with passing. However, your arms will be near your body as you contact the ball (figure 7.1*c*). This will help you absorb the shock of the attack.

As you dig the ball, relax your shoulders and draw them back as your hips move forward. This body action will help you absorb the speed of the attack and allow the rebounding dig to stay on your side of the net. In fact, as you practice absorbing the attack, you will see that the proper arm and body positions result in backspin on the

7.1 *(a)* **Ready position,** *(b)* **split-step,** *(c)* **absorb the attack.**

dug ball. This is exactly what you want since that backspin will help keep the ball in the air on your side of the net.

Always keep one thing in mind when playing defense: the ultimate objective is to keep the ball off the floor and on your side of the net. A good goal is to dig the ball high in the air near the middle of the court to allow time for your defensive teammates to transition to their offensive positions. The tendency is to dig every ball to the target (court zone 2 or net zone 6). The danger in making this your target for defense is that a ball dug just a foot or two over the net makes a wonderful gift for your opponent. Opposing attackers can blast a poorly controlled dig right back at you. It is better to be less accurate with digs away from the target than over the net.

Don't be surprised if you have very little time to communicate with teammates prior to digging a ball. Do your best to call "mine" so teammates are aware that you can play the ball. Additionally, try to call "tip" whenever you see an attacker using an off-speed shot. Limited reaction time creates a great challenge for communication on defense, so work on your ability to anticipate what the offensive player intends to do.

DIGS TO THE SIDE

To dig a ball hit just out of your reach on either side, you only need to move one arm. Drop the inside shoulder of the arm away from the ball and bring that arm and hand together with your other arm and hand to make your platform (figure 7.2). Your goal is to make adjustments with your hips, shoulders, and arms to create an effective angle for the ball to rebound under control to a target. If you combine this movement with a lateral shift of weight, attempting to get your hips behind the attacked ball, you will discover that your arms will be ready to keep the ball in play instead of the ball going out of bounds.

7.2 **Digging to the side.**

EXECUTING THE RUN-THROUGH

Players defending a tip will need to move forward to play the ball, but the goal is to stay on your feet! All too often, younger players fall to the floor unnecessarily instead of taking a big step forward; developing the run-through can help you avoid that. The term *run-through* relates to the continuous movement of a defender keeping the feet moving through and after the actual contact of the ball on the arms. To execute the run-through, stay low as you move forward and create a platform with your arms extended in front of you (figure 7.3). Continue to move through contact of the ball, and remember the goal is to pop the ball up on your own side of the net.

When moving straight toward the net, you may need to use what is called a J-stroke when contacting the ball. As shown in figure 7.4, from a side view, the arms form the letter J. This is one of the few times when you do not keep your platform straight when contacting the ball. By bending your elbows during contact, you will be able to create some backspin on the ball, increasing your chances of keeping the ball on your own side of the net.

7.3 Run through contact.

7.4 J-stroke.

USING THE SPRAWL

Our focus to this point has been on digging the ball and remaining on your feet. In certain situations, though, you need to leave your feet and go to the floor to make a save. Let's consider these situations emergencies when urgent action is needed. Diving, rolling, or sprawling on the floor all qualify as urgent actions on the volleyball court. Diving and rolling are advanced floor emergency skills that can easily cause injury if executed incorrectly. Let's look at a skill that will allow you to collapse to the floor from your defensive ready position: the sprawl.

The purpose of the sprawl is to be able to step and slide forward to cover ground quickly, make a play on the ball, then safely recover to the floor. The sprawl can be an effective skill to use if an attacker uses a tip or a roll shot or if the ball comes off the block and begins to fall just behind the blockers and in front of a defender.

To practice the sprawl, assume the defensive ready position. In slow motion, step forward with one foot, keeping both elbows inside your knees (figure 7.5a). Simply walk yourself forward on your hands until you are on the ground. Repeat this again, but this time concentrate on the position of your legs. The leg you are pushing off with as you walk yourself forward should end up straight when you are on the floor. You will be stepping with the opposite foot, so be sure that the leg of the stepping foot hits the floor on the inside of the knee. This leg needs to end up in a bent position when you are on the floor. Continue this drill until you can walk yourself forward on your hands and end up with the pushing leg straight and the stepping leg bent. The final step in this progression is to get low, take a big step simulating playing the ball (figure 7.5b), and slide forward with the outside part of your hands along the ground. This movement is not a crash to the floor but rather a collapse (figure 7.5c).

It won't take long to get comfortable going to the floor. Add a quick running step once you feel confident. As you step, simulate the action of digging a ball in front of you just before you collapse and sprawl forward. The defensive skill is the contact of the ball on your arms, and the sprawl is the emergency or the recovery skill (i.e., the ability to get yourself safely to the floor once you have let your body go off balance and left your feet). This is true of any emergency skill—the defensive skill is contacting the ball, and the skill that allows you to land safely and get back on your feet is the recovery from that action.

When the ball is way out of your range, you can use the sprawl to slide across the floor and extend your hand, palm down, across the floor. By sliding your hand just under a ball that is inches from striking the floor, you can make an exciting save. The ball will pop back in the air off the back of your hand. This is called a pancake. Clearly, this is a last-resort technique, but with practice, you will be prepared to react instantly in a situation that seems hopeless to keep the ball off the floor.

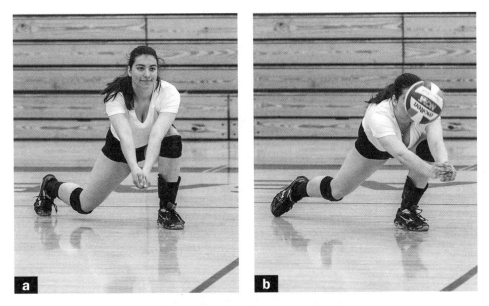

Can You Dig It?

Don't confuse the split-step position on defense with your body position when contacting the ball on a dig. If you assume the contact position before the ball is attacked, you will find yourself with your weight back on your heels. This will mean trouble for any situation in which the attacker decides to use an off-speed shot (the tip and roll shots). Keep your shoulders forward prior to contact as you read the attacker's shoulders and consider the angle of approach. These cues will help you anticipate the location of attack. You need to place yourself outside the area of the court taken away by the block in front of you. You want to get a good look at the attacker, so don't play behind the blockers. Be sure to move where you can see the attacker (figure 7.6).

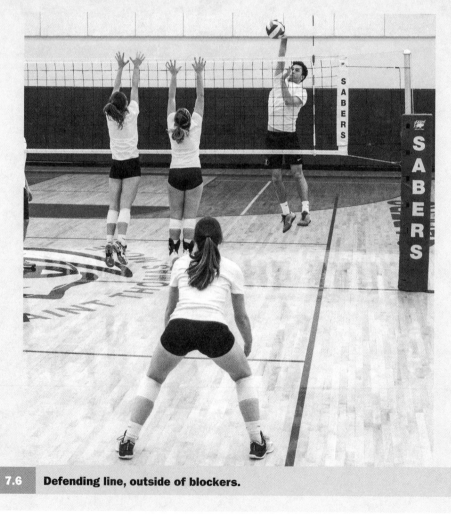

7.6 Defending line, outside of blockers.

THREE-PERSON PEPPER

The three-person pepper drill (figure 7.7) is a good way to get dig, set, and attack repetitions. Groups of three players use available space on the courts. Players A and B stand at least 15 feet (5 m) apart. Player C stands an equal distance from both players but slightly off to one side of the straight line formed by players A and B. Player A begins by hitting a down ball at player B. Player B digs the ball to player C, who sets it back to player B. Player B hits a down ball to player A, who digs the ball to player C. Player C sets the ball right back to player A. The sequence repeats for two minutes. After two minutes, all three players switch roles.

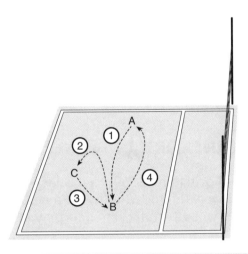

7.7 Three-person pepper.

SERVE AND DIG

Now you have the chance to combine skills to practice digging. Set up three cones in the backcourt on the serving side, one near each sideline and one near the endline (figure 7.8). Place a basket of volleyballs near the net. A coach, who will act as an attacker, stands near the basket of balls. Six servers line up behind the endline, and five other players collect the volleyballs and return them to the servers and coach. One player serves as a target. The first server executes a serve, then moves in front of one of the cones. The coach hits a down ball to the server to simulate an attack, and the server digs

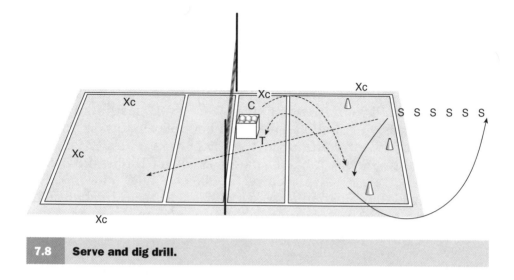

the attack toward the target stationed at the attack line. The server returns to the end of the line of servers as the next player serves. After five minutes, the target and collectors switch roles with the servers.

SETTER DIGGING DRILL

Here is a situational drill (figure 7.9) that allows setters to focus first on defending, then working together to get a set to a teammate. Two attackers on side B will alternate on each play and work on tipping

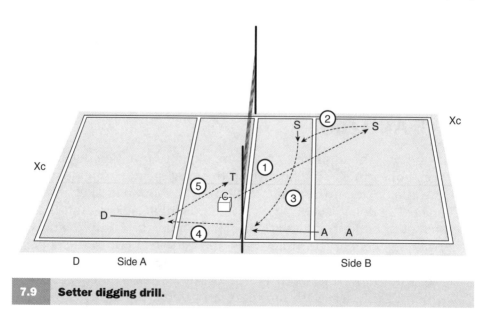

7.9   **Setter digging drill.**

84

to zone 1. Two defenders on side A will alternate on each play by digging the tip attack to a target. A coach on a box on side A initiates play by attacking at either right-side player on side B, who digs to their teammate. This player then sets to the zone 4 attacker. The target and collectors retrieve volleyballs and feed the coach with a ball as needed and after five minutes should switch roles with the attackers and defenders, while the side B right-side players switch front- and back-row positions.

CROSS-COURT PEPPER

For a cooperative drill focusing on digging, where players on each side work together to sustain a rally, start with a setter on each side of the net (figure 7.10). Two additional players are on each side of the court (court zones 4 and 5), along with two more players on each side forming a line behind the endlines. A coach tosses a ball to the side A setter, who delivers a set to the zone 4 attacker, who must get a jump and swing and attack crosscourt. The side B players react by digging the ball to their setter, who sets to the zone 4 attacker, who must now jump and swing to a side A defender. A successful dig back to the setter completes one cycle. Each time a successful attack crosses the net, the zone 4 player on that side runs to the end of the opponent's endline and joins that line, while the zone 5 player moves to zone 4 and a player from the endline steps into zone 5. The exact same rotation is continuously happening on the other side of the net as well. The teams call out their score for each successful

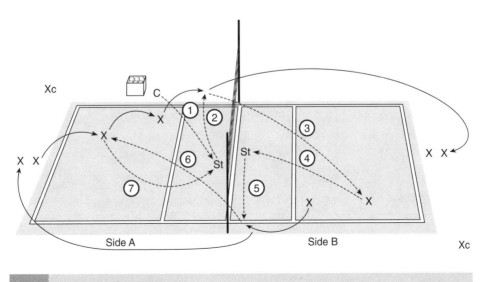

7.10 Cross-court pepper.

cycle, with a goal of 10. When an error occurs, the players balance the drill, and the coach initiates the next ball to the setter. Two or more players can help by collecting volleyballs during the drill and placing them in the basket. The teams are given 10 attempts to successfully complete 10 cycles. At the conclusion of that round, players collecting balls swap places with someone in the drill.

DEFENSE VERSUS BACK-ROW ATTACK

Game-like situations are the best way to practice. This drill allows players to practice digging while moving through situations they will see in a game. Three players line up on side A in court zones 5, 6, and 1, with another player positioned behind each of them but off the court behind the endline (figure 7.11). One player stands near the net as a target for the diggers on side A. Three players on side B take court zone positions 5, 6, and 1, with another player behind each of them. These players are the attackers. One player is the setter on side B. A coach bounces a ball high above side A, and a digger must give a free ball to the opponent. A side B attacker passes the free ball to the setter, who can set an A, B, or C back-row attack. The attacker hits deep into side A and moves into one of the digging lines on side A. The defensive players react to the ball, and one player digs the ball to the target. The digger becomes the next target. The target retrieves the ball, places it in the basket, and moves to side B to become a back-row attacker. Every two minutes, a new player is selected to be the setter.

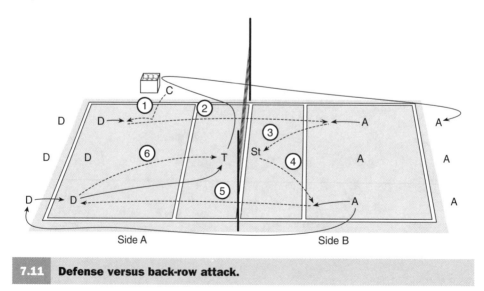

7.11 Defense versus back-row attack.

CHAPTER

The Libero

There is an exception to the substitution process you reviewed in the brief highlights of rules included in the introduction. You may have observed in a volleyball match that a back-row player on either team wearing a uniform contrasting in color from that of their teammates substitutes freely between rallies. Each team is allowed to designate one player prior to the start of each set as their libero. The term comes from the Italian for "free." This free substitute is allowed unlimited entries for any back-row player but is required to remain out for a minimum of one rally upon leaving the court.

In the late 1990s, the libero position was officially introduced for international competition and was first used for NCAA women's volleyball in the 2002 season. I remember that season well. I spent a lot of time considering each player's skills (serve receive and defense) and attributes (ball control skills and quickness) to determine how best to utilize this new role.

I recall that coaches at the time speculated that one reason the libero was introduced was to give shorter players a bigger role in the game, even though from the outset no height requirements were attached to the rule. Initially, this designated back-row player was not allowed to serve, so I immediately considered our top defensive players and passers for this role. I quickly discovered that positioning the libero after our pass and set to cover our attacker was vital in keeping balls blocked by our opponent off the floor. Without question, the introduction of the libero to our sport affected systems of team coverage (which will be introduced in chapter 11) and many other aspects of team play. Over time, on-court leadership responsibilities and potential also made my short list of considerations for selecting players for this position.

A decade of recruiting, selecting, training, and coaching liberos informs my view today that the traits of self-confidence, effective nonverbal and verbal communication, and a lively personality can also enhance the effectiveness of players in this key position. Speaking of communication, you may be asking, "Do I say (LEE-bah-ro) or (la–BEAR–oh)?" The first is most common, but both are used.

You can do it

Playing the Libero Position

There are five key rules associated with the libero:

1. The libero is restricted to performing as a back-row player.
2. The libero cannot block or attempt to block.
3. The libero is not allowed to complete an attack hit from anywhere on the court when, at the moment of contact, the ball is entirely higher than the top of the net.
4. No player may complete an attack hit on a ball from any position on the court when, at the point of contact, the ball is higher than the top of the net and if the ball came from an overhand finger pass by a libero in the front zone (on or in front of the attack line).
5. Depending on the conference or level of play, the libero may not be allowed to serve.

Initially, when the libero position was created, the libero was not allowed to serve at all. Liberos have no limit to entries, but each time they exit, they must remain out for a minimum of one play, unless they move to the position to serve for another player. In conferences that allow the libero to serve, they are limited to serve for any player but only in one rotation. While the libero can freely replace a back-row player between rallies, an assistant scorer is used to track the re-entry on a libero tracking sheet throughout each set to ensure the libero replaces the last teammate with whom they switched.

In figure 8.1, the libero has been off the court during the term of service by a middle hitter and is now legally entering in exchange for that teammate who has ended their term of service (notice the team's second middle hitter is currently in zone 4). By rule, both the libero entering the game and the teammate leaving the court must exchange across the sideline behind the attack line.

When the libero is allowed to serve, that term of service is limited to one rotation during each set. The libero in figure 8.2, who has been on the court for three rotations for the middle hitter who had previously served, is moving to the service area to serve. She is serving in place of the team's second middle hitter, who is legally exchanging places with their teammate, who is re-entering the game.

8.1   **Libero entering the court.**

8.2   **The libero stays on the court for term of service; middles exchange freely.**

ASSISTING THE BACK-ROW SETTER

As will be outlined in chapter 11 (Team Offense), at times a team has a back-row setter running the offense, which also means they are defending in the back court. As shown in figure 8.3, a back-row setter is digging the line shot, and because she will have the first team contact, another player needs to be ready to take the second touch and get the ball to an eligible attacker. Often, teams will establish the libero for this role. The back-row setter will intentionally dig the ball high to the middle of the court, and the libero will quickly move in to deliver the ball to an attacker.

8.3   **Back-row setter digs to libero.**

In figure 8.4a, the libero has both feet clearly behind the attack line at the moment of setting with his hands to a front-row attacker. The attacker in this scenario is legally permitted to attack the ball that is higher than the net.

In figure 8.4b, the libero has both feet in contact with the floor in front of the attack line and uses the arms to deliver a ball to a front-row attacker. By not using hands to set in this scenario, the attack will be legal on a ball that is above the height of the net.

8.4 *(a)* Libero legally setting front-row attacker, *(b)* libero legally passing second touch (with arms) to front-row attacker.

Teammates can assist the libero and attackers during rallies as described above, with communication commands based on their ability to see if the libero has been able to keep both feet behind the attack line when using hands to take the second contact. A teammate could shout "no hands" to the libero, indicating the need for the libero to use arms to get the ball to an attacker, or teammates may call out "no jump" to the attacker receiving a hand set from their libero, who has a foot on or in front of the attack line when contacting the ball with their hands.

Take it to the court

Libero Second-Touch Drill

Figure 8.5 shows a game-like drill where side A receives the serve to start every play and purposefully tips or hits a roll shot at the side B back-row setter on each first swing attempt. The back-row setter will intentionally dig the ball high to the middle of the court and behind the attack line to the libero, who will be responsible to get a front-row attacker a jump and swing. The libero will use their hands or arms depending on where their feet are contacting the floor in relation to the attack line at the moment of contact with the ball. Play continues to a natural conclusion, with each counterattack from side A required to be a purposeful tip or roll to the side B back-row setter.

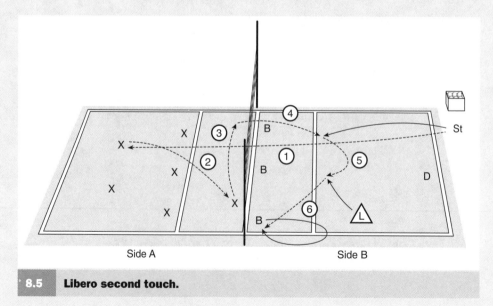

8.5 **Libero second touch.**

LIBERO VERSUS LIBERO IN 4S

Figure 8.6*a* illustrates a helpful method for allowing liberos to stay on the court all the time in a 4v4 activity while competing on the scoreboard against each other. The game can be played to 25 points with two liberos playing in court zone 5 on each side of the net. All attacks throughout this game must come from the back-row players in court zones 1 and 6.

Each libero starts with three teammates for this 4v4 drill. All other players are in one of three short lines behind the side A endline preparing to enter (three at a time) at the end of each rally. The first rally is initiated by a serve from side A's court zone 1 (right back) player. For all subsequent rallies, one player enters in this role to initiate a rally with a serve, a second player moves to zone 3 and will be a blocker and setter, and the remaining teammate enters zone 6. These new players entering the drill join the side A libero (playing in zone 5), who earns a point each time side A wins a rally. Side B, as shown, is always preparing to receive serve to start each new play, with their libero in zone 5; two teammates in zones 1 and 6, ready to pass and then be available to swing out of the back row; and one last teammate in court zone 3 in the role of blocker/setter. The side B libero earns a point each time side B wins a rally.

As shown in figure 8.6*b*, the side B libero just won a point on her scoreboard and keeps her three teammates (X_1). The three side A players (X_2) who lost the rally move back to the lines beyond the endline, while the side A libero is joined by three new teammates (X_3).

If side A wins the rally (figure 8.6*c*), that libero gets a point and three new teammates (X_3), while the three side A rally winners (X_2) quickly move to side B to replace the three players who just lost the rally. The three side B players being replaced move to the end of the lines behind the endline of side A and await their next entry when they get to the front of the line.

When either libero is the first to 13 points, the liberos change sides, and as they change, their points on the scoreboard go with them. Any advantage over being on the side that serves or receives each time is now nullified, and the first libero to 25 is the winner.

To enhance the opportunity of the designated liberos to touch the ball and have the greatest impact on the outcome of each rally, an additional rule could be put in place to require the side A libero to serve every time to the side B libero. It might be helpful to use hot spot floor markers from the side B centerline to the endline (see figure 8.7) to create a target zone for the server representing half of the space on side B. The side B libero would be required to take

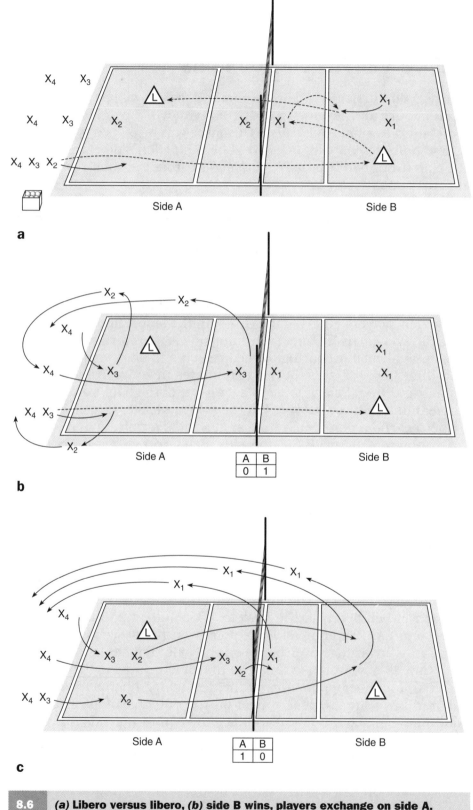

8.6 *(a)* Libero versus libero, *(b)* side B wins, players exchange on side A, *(c)* side A wins, players exchange from side A to side B.

all of these serves. A serve by the side A libero landing on the floor outside of this zone would be a point to side B.

What about scoring for the remaining players? As long as all players returning to the endline behind side A do not play each rally with the same teammates (an odd number of non-liberos helps), every player could keep their own scoreboard throughout play by keeping track of every rally they participate in that earns a point. In this way, you could determine the highest point total for all non-liberos rotating through the drill.

As with many drills, you can easily tailor this one. In chapter 12, you will see a 6v6 variation of libero versus libero that will highlight the need for liberos to constantly move with the ebb and flow of the game in a highly specialized position that will require them to pass serves, dig thunderous attacks, run down roll shots, defend all areas on and off the court with relentless pursuit, cover attackers to keep blocked balls off the floor, receive free balls, step in on the second touch when back-row setters dig the ball, and even hit down balls or deceptively place third team contacts back to the opponents when called upon.

That list of duties really just reflects the play of the game. Liberos are often called upon to be a coach on the floor to ensure that all teammates are in the correct court position for each serve to avoid overlap violations. On top of that, momentum changes start somewhere, and often the libero making an exceptional and exciting play to help their team win a long rally sets that in motion. Next time you play, take a shot at this position.

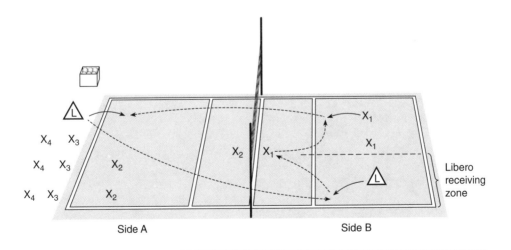

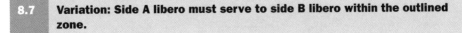
8.7 **Variation: Side A libero must serve to side B libero within the outlined zone.**

References

NCAA. 2016. *2016 and 2017 NCAA Women's Volleyball Rules and Interpretations.* Accessed May 30, 2017. www.ncaapublications.com/productdownloads/VBR17 .pdf.

Oden, B. 2017. "The Libero in Volleyball: A Defensive Specialist." Last modified August 16, 2017. www.thoughtco.com/libero-position-indoor-volleyball-3429244.

USA Volleyball. 2017. *2017-19 Indoor Domestic Competition Regulations.* Accessed May 30, 2017. https://volleyballreftraining.com/rules_interpretations_ indoor_dcr.php

Volleyball World Wide. n.d. "The Libero Volleyball Player." Accessed December 22, 2017. www.volleyball.org/rules/libero.html.

Wikipedia. 2018. "Libero." Last modified January 11, 2018. https://en.wikipedia .org/wiki/Libero.

Team Defense

Imagine an activity class playing six on six on the first day of class. It looks just like backyard volleyball. Whether their team is serving or receiving, front-row players typically stand three to five feet (1 to 2 m) away from the net. Back-row players generally stand 15 to 20 feet (5 to 6 m) away from the net in a straight line across the court. Before long, the teams are merely batting the ball back and forth over the net. Occasionally, a gung ho leader emerges on a team, suggesting they get the ball to the middle front person so that player can set or that they use all three legal contacts. What is missing from this scene is a system of play.

Systems of play will be introduced in chapters 9 to 12, which will allow you to understand court positioning responsibilities both offensively and defensively. Each play begins with a serve, which immediately puts the serving team on defense, so that is where we will begin. Let's start with an important question: Where's your base on defense? It is important to have a starting defensive position on defense; this is referred to as base position.

Defend by standing within an arm's length of the net in the ready blocking position. As a back-row player in court zones 1 or 5, begin on the attack line a few steps in from the sideline. If you are in court zone 6, start in the middle of the endline a step or two into the court. Back-row players form a triangle as shown in figure 9.1.

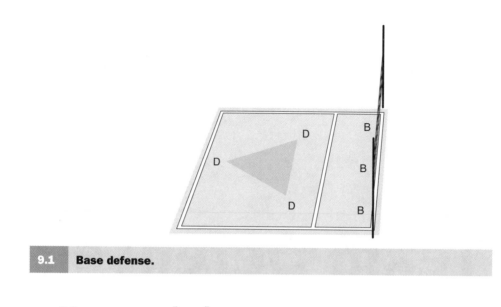

You can do it

Defending the First and Second Contact

When we think of team defense, we tend to start by thinking about how we will handle the ball set to an attacker, but that is getting ahead of ourselves. Once the serve is put in play, each defensive player must find the ball as it is being received by the opponent and be ready to react if the ball is returned immediately over the net. The overpass may not be what your opponent intends, but it happens, and the defense must be prepared to respond. This is the first opportunity for a defensive play.

The blockers have the first chance to play the ball and must prepare to defend against the overpass. Use a blocking motion for overpasses that travel high and drop down tight to the net. For the overpass that clears the net by a foot or two, quickly jump and attack the ball, and for those traveling a bit further that would otherwise land in your attack zone, simply step back and use your hands to set that ball to your setter (figure 9.2).

9.2   **Blocker versus overpass:** *(a)* **block the overpass,** *(b)* **attack the overpass,** *(c)* **step back and set the overpass.**

If the ball travels over the blockers' heads, the back-row defenders get to play defense. The back-row defenders must have the entire court covered. The players in court zones 1 and 5 can split the court from sideline to sideline and take any ball that comes over the net near the middle of the court. The player in court zone 6 can cover the deep areas of the court.

When your opponent passes the ball to a setter, the defense must prepare for the opponent's second touch to be directed over the net, either intentionally or unintentionally. The blocker must be ready to play the ball at the net. Blockers should look at the setter when the ball is in the setter's hands. The setter has the option of dumping the ball over with one hand, two hands, or even with a jump and tip or swing if the setter is a legal front-row player. The base position of your blockers and defenders enables them to defend this situation.

We have looked at how front- and back-row defenders should handle the opponent's first or second touch if it is directed over the net. Now we are ready to move on to concepts involving the blockers and defenders working together as a unit.

Most of the time when an opponent uses all three contacts, the final touch will be an attack. From the base position, back-row defenders must react to the opponent's set and move to defend against an opponent's attack from court zones 4, 2, and 3. We will refer to this defensive system as "middle back" since the defender in court zone 6 stays deep. The blockers are positioned to take the middle of the court away from the attacker, forcing the attacker to hit around them. Defensive teammates move into areas of the court not taken away by the blockers.

COURT ZONE 4 ATTACK

Against a court zone 4 attack, the outside blocker stays in front of the hitter, and the middle blocker joins the outside blocker to put a double block in front of the attack (figure 9.3). The off-blocker in court zone 4 doesn't stay at the net but retreats to a position near the attack line to retrieve any sharp-angle attacks. The defender directly behind the blocker in court zone 1 moves from base position to the sideline to dig a ball hit down the line. This player also must be ready to protect against any tips over the block. The crosscourt defender in court zone 5 moves against the sideline to defend the crosscourt attack. The player in court zone 6 stays deep in the court behind the block to cover any ball that comes over the block or travels deep down either sideline.

9.3 **Defending a court zone 4 attack (middle back defense).**

COURT ZONE 2 ATTACK

To defend a court zone 2 attack, the team's defensive positioning mirrors the positioning for defending a court zone 4 attack. The outside blocker in court zone 4 stays in front of the hitter, and the middle blocker joins the outside blocker to put a double block in front of the attack (figure 9.4). The off-blocker in court zone 2 retreats to a position near the attack line to retrieve any sharp-angle attacks.

The defender directly behind the blocker in court zone 5 moves from base position to the sideline to dig a ball hit down the line. This player also must be ready to protect against any tips over the block. The crosscourt defender in court zone 1 moves against the sideline to defend the crosscourt attack. The player in court zone 6 stays deep in the court behind the block to cover any ball that comes over the block or travels deep down either sideline.

9.4 Defending a court zone 2 attack (middle back defense).

COURT ZONE 3 ATTACK

To defend a court zone 3 attack, one option is for the middle blocker to take solo responsibility for blocking (figure 9.5), while both off-blockers move in a low position near the attack line to defend against tips, rolls, or balls deflected off the blocker's hands. The two wing defenders in zones 1 and 5 guard their sidelines. The player in court zone 6 stays deep to cover any ball hit over the block or deep into the corners.

As you gain experience, a variation to consider would be for a right- or left-side blocker to join the middle and attempt to take away more of the court, which would in turn create changes for all nonblockers in terms of space to defend.

9.5 Defending a court zone 3 attack (middle back defense).

BACK-ROW ATTACK

Do you remember the back-row attack option introduced in chapter 5? Legally positioned players in the back row can attack as long as they jump with both feet behind the attack line to attack a ball above the net. Defending the back-row attack presents a new challenge.

The blocker in front of the attacker must delay his jump slightly since the ball is being attacked from the backcourt. Compared to an attack near the net, the back-row attack takes a little longer to clear the net. The blocker's timing is important on this play. The three back-row defenders all move deep, and the two front-row players who are not involved in the block should move to a low position near the attack line to defend against deflected attacks or off-speed shots (figure 9.6).

These are the basic defensive positions and tactics for a middle back defense. Every defense has a weakness; the middle of the court is vulnerable with this type of defense. Players must guard the perimeter of the court first and move to retrieve any ball hit in front of them. The game of volleyball requires anticipation. Players must be able to read what the opponent is doing and react to each situation.

9.6 **Defending a back-row attack.**

MIDDLE UP DEFENSE

At times, an opponent may try to gain the upper hand with an off-speed attack against a middle back defense. In this case, we can easily adjust by moving the player in court zone 6 behind the middle blocker on every play (figure 9.7). This player should stay just behind the attack line in order to see the attacker's hands. In this middle up defense, the court zone 6 player would then be responsible for all tips and roll shots.

The wing defenders in this middle up system should move deeper along their sidelines since they no longer have responsibility for moving to cover off-speed attacks. The middle back part of the court will be vulnerable, placing added responsibility on the blockers to take this part of the court away from the attacker.

You will learn about other defensive systems as you move into higher levels of competitive play, and all are designed based on the responsibilities for each specialized position on the court. We will now take a closer look at how setters, liberos, middles, and pin hitters are organized in a lineup and then utilized for their specific position.

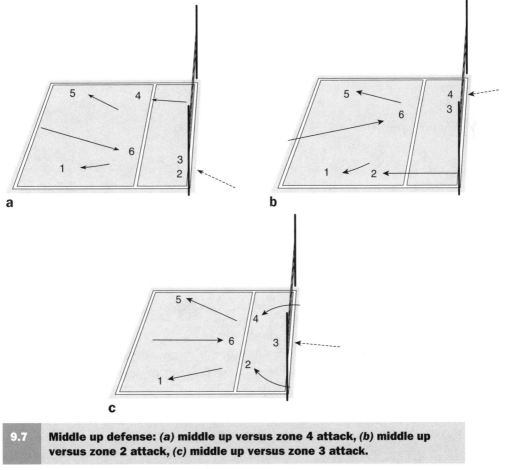

a

b

c

9.7 Middle up defense: *(a)* middle up versus zone 4 attack, *(b)* middle up versus zone 2 attack, *(c)* middle up versus zone 3 attack.

Defensive Specialization

Specialization in volleyball represents a step up from introductory play to a more advanced level. But just imagine how you'll be able to skunk your cousins at the next family reunion!

Specialization is another way to enhance the level of play on the court, as you will see when we get to chapter 11, Team Offense. Playing designated, or specialized, positions requires an understanding of where your legal position on the court is in each rotation at the moment of serve. So, let's start by assigning positions and uniform numbers to each player and identify where they begin on the court and what positions they play. Figure 9.8*a* shows the first rotation.

Notice that in the legal initial court positions, left-side players (diamonds) begin opposite each other in the rotation, as do the setters/right-side players (circles). Two designated middles (squares) also begin opposite each other, and you will notice that a libero (player 13, triangle) has replaced the back-row middle player (player 12). Remember, players must be in legal court positions at the moment of service.

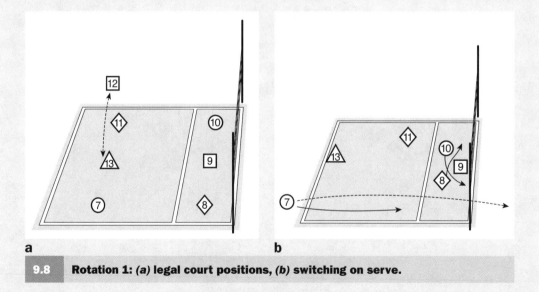

a   b

9.8   **Rotation 1: *(a)* legal court positions, *(b)* switching on serve.**

Just prior to serve, players 10 and 8 (who need to switch to their specialized position) are as close to each other as legally possible (refer back to overlap rules presented in the Introduction). They keep to either side of player 9 at the moment of serve, but since they know they will be switching, they prepare by planning for the shortest possible movement to their defensive positions.

At the serve, player 10 (right-side player) moves to court zone 2 and player 8 (left-side player) moves to court zone 4. This switch puts the team into specialized positions. Both diamonds are now on the left side, the circled setters/right-side players are both on the right, with the front-row middle and back-row libero in between.

Keep in mind that at the end of each rally, players must return to their legal court positions prior to the next serve.

Let's take a look at one more rotation (figure 9.9). In rotation 2, front-row players 10 and 9 need to switch at the moment of serve, so they take a pre-serve position (figure 9.9b) that allows that to happen quickly. Since the left-side hitter (player 8) is serving, and not legally on the court, players 7 and 13 do not have to consider any overlap rules related to that teammate and are able to assume their specialized positions prior to the service contact. Notice that our server has chosen to serve just off the court behind zone 5 to make it easier to step in to play defense on the left side of the court.

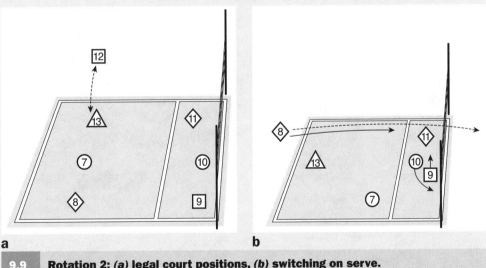

a   b

9.9   Rotation 2: *(a)* legal court positions, *(b)* switching on serve.

We'll come back to our rotations in chapter 11, Team Offense, where it will get a little more complex when we look at how to switch to specialized positions when we are the receiving team.

Defensive Teamwork

You may see teams use more than two players to block. A triple block (figure 9.10) creates a risk–reward dynamic for a defense. As you can imagine, six hands in front of a hitter can be quite effective in taking a lot of the court away from the attacker. On the other hand, it exposes more undefended area that could be inviting for an attacker to exploit with a tip or a roll shot. At the same time, balls deflected off those hands need to be chased down by nonblockers, who must be alert and ready to move.

Team defense requires a lot of discipline because each player has a predetermined area of responsibility. However, sometimes the ball is attacked in the seam between two players. (Figure 7.9, setter digging drill, provides an example.) Players need to be able to work together so they do not collide. The seam digging drill illustrates this type of situation.

9.10 Triple block.

SEAM DIGGING

In the seam digging drill (figure 9.11), adjacent defenders practice moving to dig a ball hit in the seam between them. Three players begin in a blocking line near court zone 4, while three other players form a digging line near court zone 5. The first blocker and defender in line begin in base defense position. When the coach on a box across the net in zone 4 tosses the ball in the air, both defenders move to their middle back defensive positions and prepare to dig the attack from the coach. The coach aims the ball between the players so they can practice moving to dig the ball; the goal is for the blocker to move inside for the ball while the defender moves behind. By moving in parallel lines, the players avoid colliding with each other. The blocker has the first chance to get to the ball. The defender has the second chance to dig the ball to the target. The blocker and defender return to their lines after each attempt, and the next players in each line come on the court. Six other players collect volleyballs, feed balls to the coach, and serve as the target. They change with the blockers and diggers after three minutes or a predetermined number of attempts.

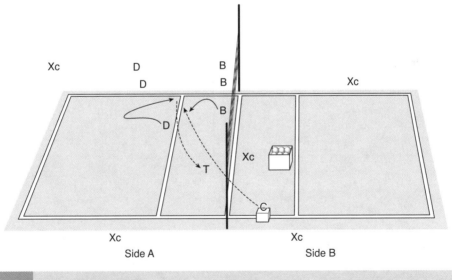

9.11 Seam digging drill.

DEFENSE VERSUS TWO LINES OF ATTACKERS

Let's practice moving from base position to defensive positions in a middle back defense (side B) against attacks from side A zones 2 or 4. In figure 9.12, the side A team starts with a designated passer, setter, and two attackers ready to rotate on the court in zones 2 and 4. A coach on side B initiates each new play by tossing a ball to the side A passer, who directs the pass to the setter. The setter has two attack options (14 or 94) available. Side B defenders begin in base positions and move into proper position for a middle back defense. They have two minutes to accumulate points based on the following criteria.

1. Side A attack error or ball blocked back to side A = plus 1

2. Side A play ending attack, untouched by side B defenders = minus 1

3. Side B touches or digs an attack before it hits the floor but can't successfully return to side A with a free ball = plus 1

4. Side B controls a dig and is able to send a free ball to side A passer = plus 2

As long as side B can dig the attack and on either their second or third contact successfully give a free ball to the side A passer, the drill continues. Whenever the ball hits the floor or goes out of

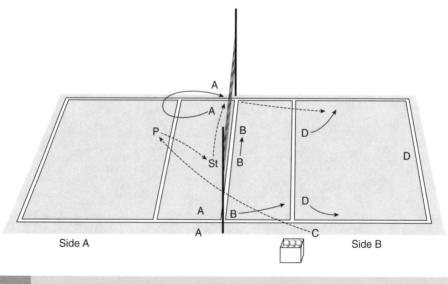

9.12 Setup for defense versus two lines of attackers.

bounds, the coach initiates the next ball. After each attack attempt, the side A attackers switch with the other teammate in their zone. The coach calls out the cumulative score throughout the two-minute period. After two minutes the teams all help collect volleyballs, then switch sides. The original side A team now plays defense and collects points for two minutes. The team with the most points wins each time period.

For a variation, side A attack options could be changed to include zone 3 and back-row attack.

BONUS BALL

Let's focus on team defense in a fast-moving, competitive situation. Six players are assigned to each side of the court in specialized positions (figure 9.13). Each team begins each rally already in those positions. Two coaches stand near each sideline with a ball cart nearby. Each coach begins with three volleyballs of the same color and one different-colored ball. Teams can play rock, paper, scissors to see who gets the first ball. The team going first, and then each successive team winning a rally, receives a free ball from their opponent. To initiate a free ball, coaches bounce a ball high above the court on their side whenever that team loses a rally. The bounced ball must be given to the opponent as a free ball. The first team to win three rallies (three volleyballs of same color) gets their different colored ball

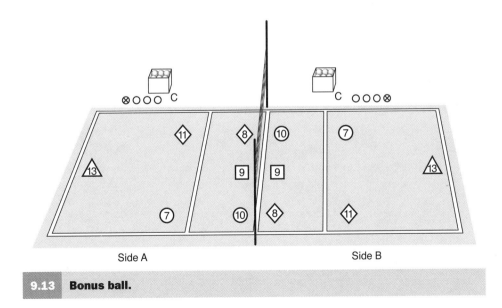

Side A   Side B

9.13 **Bonus ball.**

introduced to the drill. This bonus ball is their only chance to win in this drill. The team receiving the bonus ball wins one point if they win the rally. If the opponent wins the rally, that team immediately earns their bonus ball, which represents their only opportunity to win a point. If neither team wins on their own bonus ball, all players chase the volleyballs and prepare for the next game, with no points awarded. After a team has won three points, the front- and back-row players switch positions but remain in their specialized court zones. The first team to win six points wins the drill.

Free Ball

We just reviewed defensive systems you can use against your opponent's attacks, but what happens when the opposition struggles with controlling their first and second contacts and can't mount an attack either with a jump and swing or a down ball? The only option is to push an easier-to-defend overhead or forearm pass across the net to keep the rally going. This easier-to-defend third contact coming your way is called a free ball.

The W formation is commonly used as a basic free ball offensive system when moving from defense to offense.

Creating the W

Once a team on defense anticipates during a rally that their opponents cannot attack their third contact, they simply need to call out "free ball" and move to the W formation. This example of moving from defense to preparing to play offense is called *transition*. Transition will be covered in more detail in chapter 12, including match situations when you also move from offense to defense.

To move from base defensive positions to create a W formation (figure 10.1*a*), the player already in zone 2 as a blocker can be designated as the setter and should take a position near net zone 6. Blockers in zones 3 and 4 turn and run straight back behind the

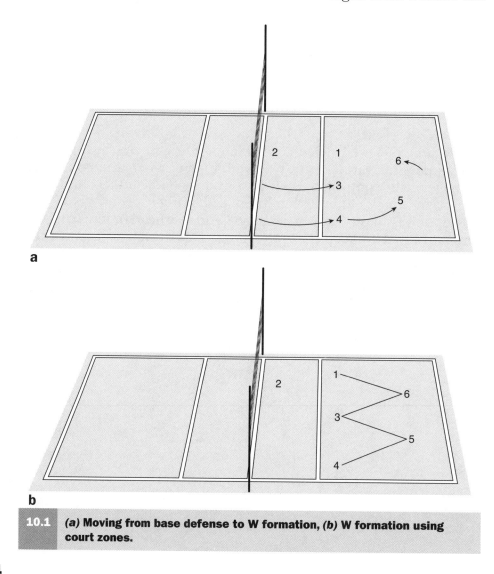

a

b

10.1 *(a)* **Moving from base defense to W formation,** *(b)* **W formation using court zones.**

attack line to prepare to attack, and now join their teammate in zone 1 to form a straight line, while teammates in zones 5 and 6 position themselves as shown in figure 10.1*b* to create the W. Five players are now in position to receive the free ball.

More to choose and use

USING THE W

The W needs to be formed before the ball crosses the net (figure 10.2). To get everyone on the same page and in position, as soon as one player calls "free," a chorus from all teammates shouting "FREE!" should activate movement from the entire team. A team that has everyone in a W prior to the ball crossing the net will increase the chances of quality first and second contacts that lead to a strong attack.

Free balls are commonplace at beginning levels when ball control skills are in the developmental stage. While less frequent at higher levels of competition, you will notice that highly skilled players show a good bit of enthusiasm when they call "free." Why? Because they realize their team has just gained the advantage in earning this point.

10.2 W formed before ball crosses the net.

Consider the challenge you have now discovered in developing your serve receive skills. Tough float and jump serves from your opponent make forearm and overhead passing quite difficult. Receiving a free ball is a welcome relief during a match, so take advantage of that on the first contact.

Use your hands to receive a free ball (figure 10.3) whenever possible. Your goal is to deliver an accurate first contact right to the setter, so practice using your hands to accomplish this.

10.3 Free ball received with hands.

When you are in court zones 3 and 4, keep in mind the end goal is for you to get a strong swing on this play. One potential team strategy is limiting your first contact touches to free balls that could land inside your attack line, relying heavily on your backcourt teammates to cover a lot of ground, and assertively calling for and handling the first touch. Then, you can focus much more on attacking. When you do take the first contact, push the ball high to the setter to give yourself ample time to run, jump, and swing.

Figure 10.4 shows the zone 5 player (libero) moving up to receive a free ball between the two attackers, who are now preparing to approach for an attack.

10.4 Back-row priority for free ball.

Let's not forget about our libero. Many elite level teams allow their libero to have first refusal on every single free ball from an opponent. If this ball control specialist is your top ball handler, this makes sense. Communication will be crucial for success when your team commits to this strategy. Liberos covering a lot of ground to contact the ball can help their teammates give way by saying "mine, mine, mine" as they travel to the ball. Figure 10.5 shows the zone 5 libero moving between zones 1 and 6 to take charge of the free ball.

10.5 Libero priority for free ball.

HANDS ONLY

This competitive 6v6 drill demands that all free ball receptions are played with the hands and places a premium on effective first and second team contacts. Additionally, the player initiating play with a free ball will be motivated to discover how to effectively send the ball to the opponent and make it difficult for them to use their hands. Side B begins in their base defensive position. Side A players start in a W formation. A coach on side A bounces a ball high and deep on side A's court simulating their second touch and forcing them to give up a free ball to side B. Once side A delivers the free ball, they move to their base defensive position. Side B players respond to the free ball by calling "free" and moving to the W prior to the ball crossing the net. Side B players must use their hands on each free ball, and the attacker must jump and swing to be eligible for the point. The team that wins the rally wins the point, and the first team to six wins. At the end of the game, the coach moves to side B, and that team will receive bounced balls while side A works on forming the W and using their hands to receive each free ball. The game continues until one team reaches six points. As shown in figure 10.6, both teams will get the chance to transition between defensive base positions and the W formation.

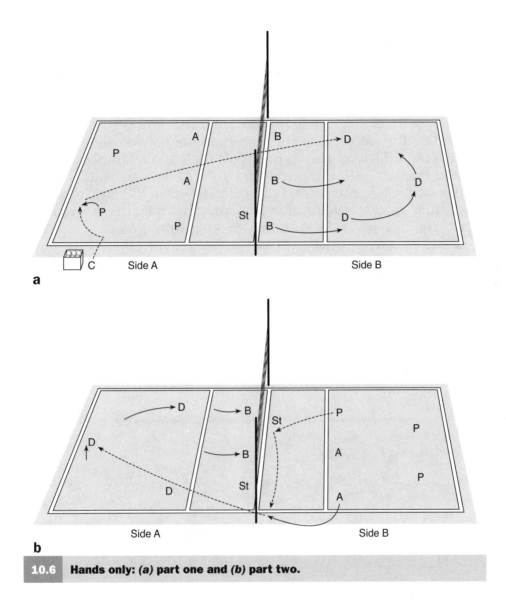

a

b

10.6 Hands only: *(a)* part one and *(b)* part two.

FREE BALL UP TEMPO

To practice first tempo and slide attacks for your middle players, this drill rewards the free ball receiving team for scoring on a 51 or 92 with their middle attacker. The team giving up the free ball gets a bonus point if they are able to counterattack and score on a 51 or 92. Use the same game rules and initiate play as shown in the hands-only drill, but now (figure 10.7) the middle attacker on side B must connect with the setter on either a 51 or 92 slide, or they automatically lose the point. When side B scores directly from a 51 or 92, they receive a point. If side A wins the rally, they receive the point, and if they win by counterattacking with a 51 or 92 slide of their own that scores, they receive two points. The coach will initiate play with a bounce on side A six times in a row and then move to side B and initiate six more rallies with a bounce on that side. The team with the highest score after 12 plays wins the game.

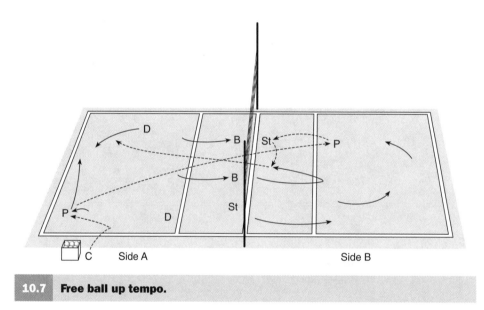

10.7 Free ball up tempo.

Team Offense

In chapter 10, you learned the basic W formation, most commonly used to receive a free ball. That formation can also be the foundation for creating a simple offensive system. In each rotation, whoever is in court zone 2 is the setter, and players in court zones 3 and 4 are the primary attackers. One benefit of this system is that all six players gain experience in each court position.

Using the W formation, as outlined above, we could actually call this a 6-6 offense because all six players are setters when they are in the front row (zone 2), and all six players are attackers when they are in the front row (zones 3 and 4).

Participants introduced to most sports typically find that they have natural strengths and weaknesses. This is true for volleyball as well. In this chapter, we will build on the specialization concepts introduced in chapter 9, applying them to offense.

Modified 4-2

Let's keep the player designations from chapter 9 (figure 9.8*a*) as we introduce our first offensive system. We can continue to use the W as the foundation of our offense, but let's add some rules. Players 7 and 10 (circles) will be designated as the setters. Our initial offensive system requires them to be setters whenever they are in the front row. This means that when the opponent serves, they need to move to the target (court zone 2, net zone 6). The remaining players must prepare for the serve receive by establishing a W formation that complies with the overlap rules, explained in the Introduction.

Since two players are designated setters, the other four players can be designated attackers when in the front row. The two front-row attackers must be prepared to attack in court zones 3 and 4 once the ball is passed. Once the serve is returned across the net, players must switch to their specialized positions.

This offensive system is referred to as an international or modified 4-2 (figure 11.1). The 4 represents the number of players designated as attackers when in the front row. The 2 represents the number of players designated as setters when in the front row. Note that in all the illustrations, the libero (player 13) has substituted in the back row for the middle players (12 and 9), who are only on the court in the front row.

You might wonder why this offense is called a modified 4-2. Many people have been exposed to some form of volleyball where the setter is the player in court zone 3 (middle front). When two players are designated setters in the front row and they perform their setting duties in court zone 3, this is referred to as a 4-2. The simple modification to this once popular system is to have the setter in court zone 2. This allows both front-row attack options to be front sets.

Switching on offense is more complicated than switching on defense because you can't switch until your team puts the ball across the net. Let's examine the first rotation in a modified 4-2 (figure 11.1*a*). The designated setter (player 10) begins near the net, which removes any chance of receiving the serve, and is slightly closer to the left sideline than player 9 to avoid an overlap violation. Notice in figure 11.1*b* that in forming the W, player 8 (right front) must stay slightly closer to the centerline than player 7 (right back). The overlap rules can be used as a guide for each offensive rotation. At the moment of service, setter 10 moves across the court to the target. Player 11 receives the serve, passing the ball to player 10. The attackers, players 8 and 9, move into position to attack the set from player 10. Player 10 sets the ball to player 9, who attacks it and sends it over the net

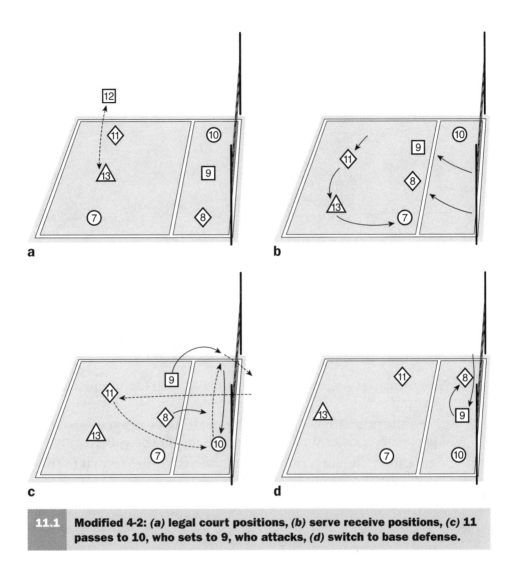

Modified 4-2: *(a)* legal court positions, *(b)* serve receive positions, *(c)* 11 passes to 10, who sets to 9, who attacks, *(d)* switch to base defense.

(figure 11.1*c*). Once the ball crosses the net, the players move into their defensive or transition positions (figure 11.1*d*), preparing to defend the attack from the opponent.

Let's look at the same rotation and make a few tactical changes: (1) our libero will defend in court zone 5, and our back-row left-side player will defend in court zone 6, and (2) our designated front-row middle will always use the 51 option from serve receive, and our designated front-row left-side player will always take their first swing on the left side. Figure 11.2*a* shows the new approach angles for players 9 and 8, but now the 14 goes to player 8. Since players 8 and 9 are now in their specialized zones, the only additional switch needed (players 13 and 11) occurs once the attack crosses the net, as shown in figure 11.2*b*.

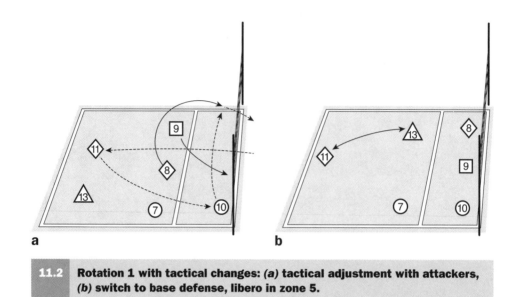

a   b

11.2 **Rotation 1 with tactical changes: *(a)* tactical adjustment with attackers, *(b)* switch to base defense, libero in zone 5.**

You can take it from here to practice the next five rotations. Just follow these rules:

1. The front-row setter starts near the net with teammates legally forming a W.

2. Once the attack has crossed the net, all players move to their specialized positions for the remainder of the rally.

3. Remember, for each rally lost, all players must return to their legal court positions to start the next play.

More to choose and use

COVERING THE BLOCKED BALL

We know what the defense is going to try to do against our attack. They want to put a wall of hands in front of our attacker and finish the play with a roof (see chapter 6). Our offense can protect our court against a blocked ball by having the five nonattacking players take part in covering the court.

Individual and team coverage can take away the potential momentum of a great block. To cover, move in a low position to surround the attacker. Keep your arms low and apart as you move to cover. Keep your eyes on the blocker's hands. Usually, if the attack is blocked back to you, you will want to use your passing platform to keep the ball off the floor. Try to get the ball high in the air and back to your offensive target in court zone 2 and net zone 6. This gives your team another opportunity in transition to get a swing at the net.

Many team coverage systems can be used. One very effective coverage system is the 3-2. Three players attempt to closely surround the attacker to prevent a blocked ball from hitting the floor near the net (figure 11.3). In most cases, the libero would be one of these three and would have a prominent covering role on each and every attack. The other two players remain deeper in the court and split the coverage of the remaining open space.

Having added this additional component of the game, we can now put it all together with our team offense.

11.3   Surround the attacker.

TRANSITION TO COVERAGE

Let's look at the transition to coverage in rotation 1 (figure 11.4). As the attacker is getting ready to send the ball across the net, the other players move to coverage positions (the 3-2). Once the ball crosses the net, they switch to specialized positions. Player 11 receives the serve, passing it to player 10, who sets a 14 to player 8 (figure 11.4a). The libero (player 13) covers the area behind the attacker, player 9 approached for a 51 and now covers near the net, while the setter (player 10) moves into the space between players 9 and 13. Players 11 and 7 split the area in the back row (3-2 coverage system for left-side attack; figure 11.4b). After the attack crosses the net, players transition from coverage to base defense (figure 11.4c).

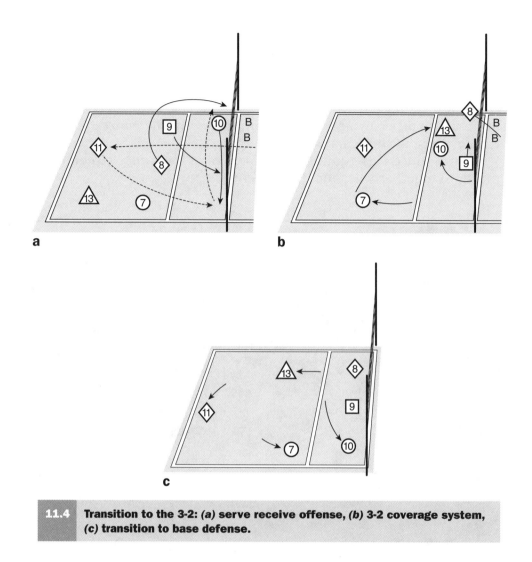

Transition to the 3-2: *(a)* serve receive offense, *(b)* 3-2 coverage system, *(c)* transition to base defense.

THE 6-2 OFFENSE

By this time, you may be wondering why we introduced the back set. Our next offensive system description will provide the answer. Let's make one small change in our modified 4-2 offense. Using the same players, we will designate our two setters for the job of setting when they are in the back row. That means the setters join the other four players as attackers when in the front row. We now have six players designated as attackers when in the front row, and two of those players have the additional job of setting when in the back row. The setter still has two attack options in front but now also has a back set option at all times. This offense is called a 6-2 (figure 11.5).

Let's also make an adjustment to our serve receive system by using only four players. If you watch accomplished teams play, you

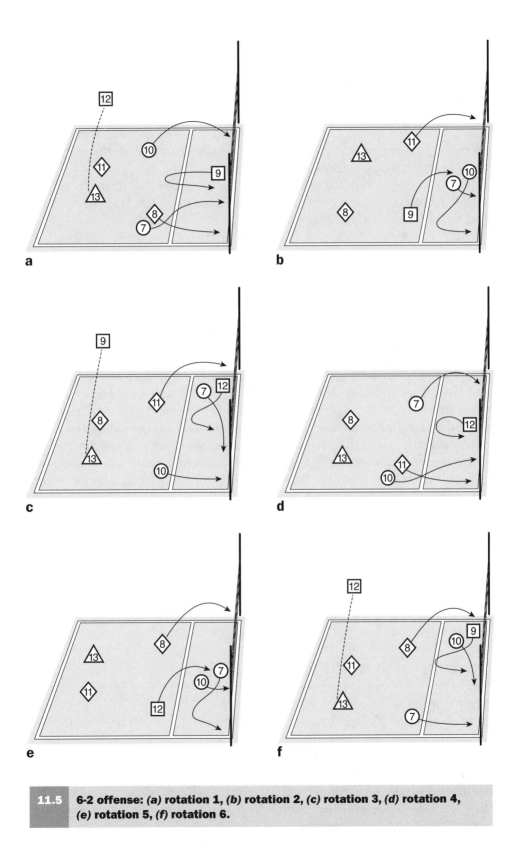

6-2 offense: *(a)* rotation 1, *(b)* rotation 2, *(c)* rotation 3, *(d)* rotation 4, *(e)* rotation 5, *(f)* rotation 6.

will likely see that they use fewer than five players to receive serve. You may ask, "Where is the W?" In each rotation below, you will see how the foundation of the W is still in place, but it is advantageous to use one less passer.

You may have noticed that the passer in the middle of the W sometimes seems to get in the way. Teams can easily require their most effective passers to cover a larger part of the court by eliminating the responsibility of passing from one or more players. The 6-2 offense (figure 11.5) provides an example of a four-passer system. In all six of the serve receive patterns, the middle of the court has opened up and will be less congested.

Since the setter in a 6-2 is legally in the back row, we need to establish the serve reception positions for each rotation to avoid overlap violations. Several advantages are gained by the move to a four-passer system: (1) the libero (likely your best passer) begins to have more court to cover, (2) the designated back-row setter is able to get as close to the net as possible prior to serve, and (3) the middle attacker in most rotations is now free to focus on first-tempo attack options.

The keys to running a 6-2 revolve around the initial court position and movement of the designated setter. The back-row setter needs to be as close to the target as possible at the moment of serve and should be prepared for the constant transitions on the court between zones 1 and 2. We will take a closer look at the transition movements of the setter in chapter 12. Strategically, we will also hide the setter, in a sense, right behind a teammate designated to receive or, even better, if legal, right behind a teammate who is at the net (see rotations 2, 3, 5, and 6) to make it nearly impossible for a serving team to get the designated setter to take the first contact.

In the first rotation, the setter (player 7) hides behind player 8. At the moment of service, the setter runs to the target before the serve crosses the net and prepares to run the offense. Following our specialization rule, the setter in a 6-2 must return to a back-row base position once the ball crosses the net to the opponent.

THE 5-1 OFFENSE

What if a team decides to use one setter all the time? All we need to do is designate player 7 to set all the time. Player 10 will no longer be a setter but just an attacker in the front row. This would create a 5-1 offense, an offense in which five players attack when they are in the front row and one player sets all the time. Essentially, a 5-1 occurs when we use a 6-2 half the time and a modified 4-2 half the time. In a 5-1 offense, the player in the rotation opposite the setter is referred to as the *opposite*.

Passing Systems

One benefit of specialization is that it allows a team to play the percentages. Allowing your best setters to set the ball or your tallest players to block in the middle increases your chances of success. This is true for serve reception as well.

As your team plays competitively, the most effective passers will begin to emerge. Instead of using four passers with varying degrees of effectiveness controlling the first contact, you can use a three-passer system (figure 11.6a). As you reduce the number of passers, you reduce seams between passers and allow the best passers more opportunities to maximize their skill.

If player 8 is the weakest passer, we could hide her near the net in our three-passer system, removing any passing responsibility. An additional benefit to this move is that our setter (player 7) is now starting closer to the target. Notice that as we remove serve receive responsibility for some players, the libero begins to take on more court space to cover.

The three passers could also split the court (figure 11.6b), aligning almost in a straight line; however, our left front player 10 must be slightly closer to the centerline than our left back player 11 (figure 11.6b). Verbal communication must be developed among the passers, and additional areas of responsibility should be assigned to handle the seams.

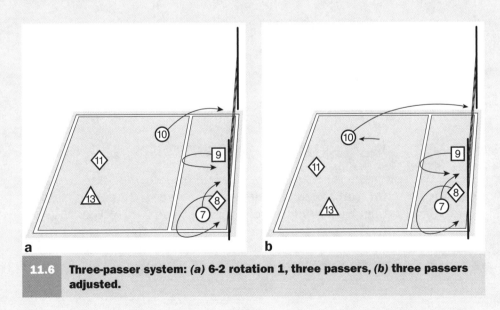

a   b

11.6 Three-passer system: *(a)* 6-2 rotation 1, three passers, *(b)* three passers adjusted.

Finally, we could move player 11 to just inside the endline and rely on two players to cover the whole court in a two-passer system (figure 11.7). Player 11 could be given the additional responsibility of calling "in" or "out" for serves traveling deep in the court, and players 8 and 9 could be on high alert to play any served ball that hits the net tape and begins to fall to the floor inside the attack line.

There are many passing system options. It is critical that players are placed on the court legally, avoiding overlap violations. Even if you use a passing system with fewer than five players, keep in mind that the W still provides a comfortable and effective formation for handling every free ball that your opponent gives you. It would not be at all unusual for a team to use a passing system with three designated passers in each rotation but continue to use the W for every free ball during transition.

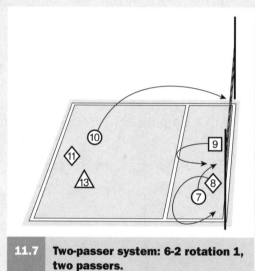

11.7 Two-passer system: 6-2 rotation 1, two passers.

In System and Out of System

These two phrases are keys to offensive systems. "In system" describes a team that receives a serve with a pass that goes right to the designated setter so accurately that setting a first tempo (e.g., 51) is an option. When the designated setter has to run so far away from the net to get to a poorly passed ball that setting a first tempo is not an option, we refer to this as "out of system."

When the setter can't get to the second touch and has to call for help (figure 4.11, the bread and butter drill), this is clearly out of system. The primary goal when you are out of system is to get a jump and swing, and often that will come from a high set to pin hitters or a set to back-row attackers.

When high-level teams are in system, you will see attackers using a combination of different tempos on the same play. You will find it most realistic to start working on combination plays on a free ball, but as your skills develop, you will want to incorporate combination plays into your offense.

In figure 11.8, a first tempo option comes from the opposite running a 71, while a second tempo option is created when the middle player runs a slide (92). This movement will activate the defensive blockers as they attempt to stay in front of these two attackers. Let's allow the left-side player to have a 14 as their option, which creates a third tempo option. Also pictured here is a player from the back row hitting a B. Advanced-level players would have a setter informing teammates before the serve of what play to run on the serve receive, along with a play like this to run if they get a free ball. Like so many sports, watching only the ball will prevent you from seeing all that is going on. Combination plays create advantages for the attackers primarily by increasing opportunities for them to face no more than one blocker.

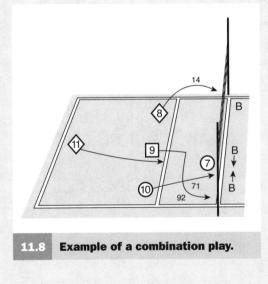

11.8 Example of a combination play.

COVERAGE DRILL

In the coverage drill (figure 11.9), you will practice moving to coverage positions by surrounding an attacker. A left-side attacker on side B starts near the zone 4 attack line and is joined by a setter and two teammates receiving serve. One server on side A will initiate the drill with a serve. Three blockers are grouped together on side A to form a triple block to increase the chances of a successful block being returned to side B. Four other players surround the court to collect balls. Side B uses a two-passer system on each serve reception, and the setter will deliver a 14 to the attacker. Once the ball is set, the setter and two passers surround the attacker. The covering players attempt to play any blocked ball high in the air, leading to another swing from the side B attacker. Whenever an attack ends the play, the side A server immediately initiates the next play with a serve. Every three minutes, the ball collectors move into side A roles, side A players move to side B, and side B collects volleyballs.

Try this variation: alternate side B attacker with a middle attacker and then a right-side attacker.

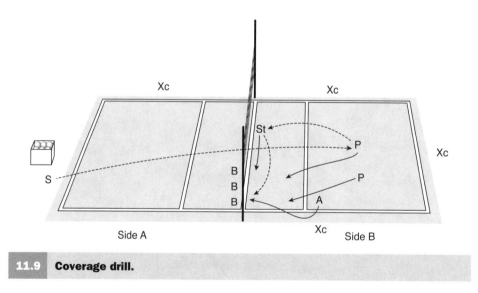

11.9 Coverage drill.

FIVE IN EACH ROTATION

In figure 11.10, six players on side B prepare to receive serve in rotation 1 of a 6-2 offense. Three blockers and three defenders are on the opposite side of the net. One of the defenders begins the drill by serving. The offensive team receives five consecutive serves, then moves to rotation 2. After the offensive team has taken five serves in each rotation, they become the serving side, and side A completes five plays in each rotation.

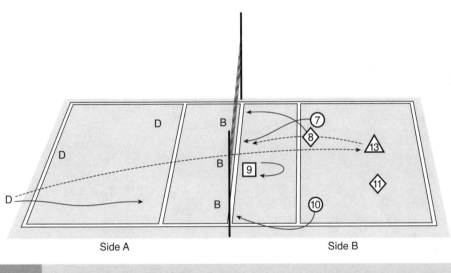

11.10 Five in each rotation drill.

CHAPTER

Transition

What is missing from most backyard volleyball scenes and many recreational games? It's transition. Transition needs to be a big part of your focus in learning how to play. If you watch accomplished players in a 6v6 competition, you will notice that the front-row players are either at the net to block or away from the net and near the attack line preparing to approach and swing.

We have established offensive systems that place players in positions to be able to receive the serve and then attack from the attack line or the back row. We have established base positions for each defender and a few defensive systems. We have also introduced the two most common transition situations: (1) free ball, and (2) covering the attacker. Now we need to consider the movement required for players to transition from defense to offense and from offense to defense.

From Defense to Offense

The first priority for transition from defense to offense is the free ball, since this is the most common situation a team will face during play.

The individual movement of players in this free ball transition is critical. Front-row blockers are positioned at the net on defense. The free ball signal requires all front-row designated attackers to retreat to the attack line. Often players will backpedal, using many small steps to arrive near the attack line. This type of movement is inefficient.

Volleyball requires running. Players need to cover five- or ten-foot (2 to 3 m) spaces quickly. Front-row players begin to transition on a free ball (figure 12.1*a*) by turning from the net, keeping their eyes on the opponent's court, and taking a long running step toward the attack line, followed by two quick smaller steps. In most cases, three running steps are all that is needed (figure 12.1*b*). Back-row defenders use a similar footwork pattern to move from their defensive base to the area of the court they are responsible for in the W. The transition movement drill (figure 12.2) allows two teams to work on these footwork patterns.

Down Ball Opportunities

A free ball opportunity occurs when an opposing player prepares to use a passing platform or hands to direct a third team contact over the net. A defensive team might also respond to a player executing a down ball (attack from the floor) on the third team contact with a free ball signal.

Blocking a down ball is not a high-percentage play. In fact, an attacker who did not jump to attack would find blocking hands above the net a very inviting target. As players gain experience, they should be encouraged to react to a down ball as a free ball.

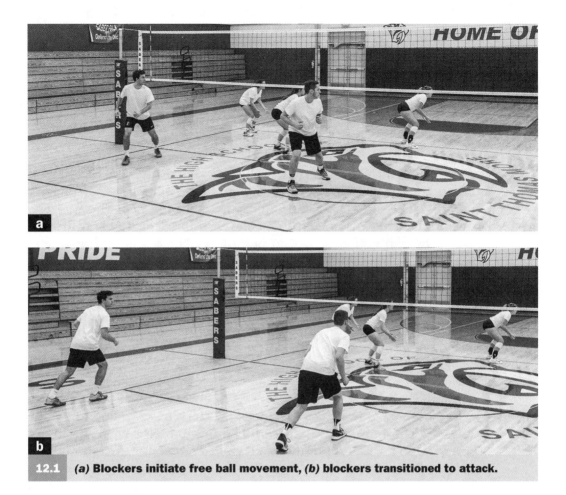

12.1 *(a)* Blockers initiate free ball movement, *(b)* blockers transitioned to attack.

Offense to Defense

Each player must also move quickly from offense to defense. Typically, this requires moving from team coverage position to base defensive position. Remember to move quickly and keep your eyes on the ball in the opponent's court throughout this transition.

Long rallies produce multiple opportunities for players to move from offense to defense. Don't get caught flat-footed when your opponent digs an attack. Remember, they have the same transition goal as you—to counter-attack! Get back to base quickly when you or a teammate are dug by the opponent, and prepare to defend your court.

THE SETTER

Transition for the back-row setter is a challenge. On defense, this player expects to dig the ball. At the same time, the setter needs to read and react quickly to every attack that is directed at a teammate. In this situation, the setter needs to release quickly to the target, prepare to move to the ball that is successfully dug, and run a transition offense. The numbering system for set height and location is extremely important in transition because the attackers need to signal the setter verbally while the ball is in the air. The setter often hears more than one player calling for a set. Although this can be confusing, it is also helpful for the setter to know who is ready to attack.

Since the setter needs to play defense at the moment of each attack, the designated setter in any offensive system is likely to be the player to dig the ball at times. One of the great benefits of specialization is that we have at least two options to consider when our setter digs an attack, at which time you will often hear that player say "setter out." In other words, the setter is now unavailable for the second touch. A setter who is also a back-row defender needs to dig the ball to the target area, allowing the right-side player in the front row (often referred to as the secondary setter) to set the ball in transition. A second option was introduced in chapter 8 with the libero second-touch drill, commonly used when a team has designated the libero for this assignment.

The designated setter in the front row may also be in a position to dig a ball, especially as an off-blocker. In this case, the setter should dig the ball high into the middle of the court so that the right-side player in zone 1 can move in to set the ball in transition. The setter digging drill (figure 7.9) is effective in training right-side players to work together in transition from digging to setting.

DIG-SET-SWING

This is the goal every time your opponent attacks. At that moment, they have the advantage. You can change all of that with a successful dig that leads to a jump and swing counterattack. The activation drill (figure 12.4) will challenge this part of your game when the only chance to earn points comes from a dig that leads directly to an attack that ends the rally.

Transition Between Skills

Players also need to work on transition movements between skills. Some drills combine two or more skills. These combination drills often simulate competitive situations while allowing repetition for skill development. Our serve and dig drill (figure 7.8) is an example of a drill combining two consecutive touches by a player. Combination drills can also be developed to utilize a series of movements and touches. The block, dig, and attack combination drill (figure 12.3) will challenge you to transition from defense to offense by combining three skills.

Give it a go

TRANSITION MOVEMENT

The transition movement drill (figure 12.2) makes you practice moving from defense to the W formation on a free ball and back to base defensive positions. Six players on side A begin in specialized base defensive positions. Six players on side B begin in specialized free ball court positions for a modified 4-2 offense. The coach signals

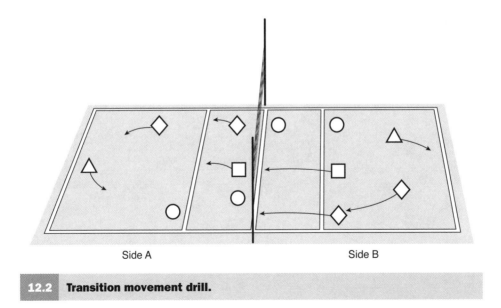

Side A   Side B

12.2 **Transition movement drill.**

"free ball," and the team on side A immediately moves to a free ball court formation while the team on side B moves to base defensive positions. The coach signals "free ball" again, and the teams quickly move back to their original court positions. The coach signals "free ball" four more times and players transition. Front- and back-row players switch positions on each team and repeat the drill.

BLOCK, DIG, AND ATTACK COMBINATION

The footwork for transitioning from blocking to digging to attacking is the focus for this drill (figure 12.3). Four players form a line on side B near court zone 4. The first player gets into a ready blocking position, with one setter in position and another setter off the court prepared to rotate in on each new play. On side A, a coach on a box is positioned near zone 4, one player with a ball is in court zone 2, and five other players prepare to collect volleyballs. The side A player will do a self-toss, then jump and attack into the blocker's hands to initiate the play. The blocker executes a block, then turns and runs to the attack line to dig a ball (attacked by the coach on the box) to the setter, then attacks to complete the three-skill sequence. The next side B blocker immediately steps in for the next play. The ball collectors feed volleyballs as needed to the coach on the box and

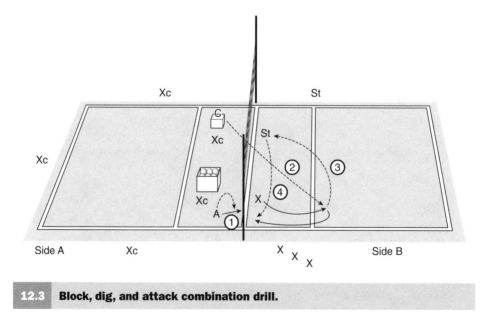

12.3　Block, dig, and attack combination drill.

the side A attacking player. The drill continues until each player on side B has had 10 attempts, then players switch sides of the net and change roles.

ACTIVATION

In this 6v6 drill, the only way to earn points is when your team earns activation. To focus on counterattacking, establish a point producing "dig-set-swing" as the criteria for either team to become activated.

Teams alternate serve whenever a rally ends with neither team being activated. When either team completes a dig-set-swing for a point, they begin to receive free balls from their opponent, and their scoreboard is activated. In the illustration below (figure 12.4), side A served and successfully counterattacked to end the rally. The coach on side B bounces the ball high above their court. This bounced ball is considered side B's second contact, and they must give a free ball to side A. If side A wins this rally, they get a point and earn another free ball. This continues until side B wins a rally, deactivating side A. Team B would serve next, which would give them the first chance for a dig-set-swing point. This game can be scored by the first team attaining a certain number of points, or it could be a timed game, with the top scoring team at the end of the time period declared the winner.

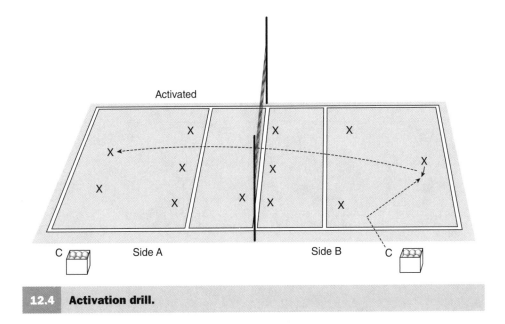

12.4 **Activation drill.**

LEFT VERSUS LEFT

Now let's practice team transition while working on all skills, with emphasis on left-side attacking. Two teams of six players are on each side of the court in specialized court positions (figure 12.5). Coaches stand close to the sidelines near court zone 5 on each side of the net. The coach on side A initiates the drill by tossing a volleyball high in the air to the setter on side A. The designated setter on side A moves to play the ball. Setters must set to the left-side attacker on each toss but can set to any other player during rallies. The drill continues until one team cannot return the ball over the net. The team that wins each rally gets the next toss. Every play results in a point for the left-side player on the winning side who is competing on the scoreboard against the opposing left-side player. The game is played until one side reaches 15 points. All players help collect volleyballs at the conclusion of each game.

Right versus right and middle versus middle are natural variations for players who specialize as opposites or middles.

Two scoring modifications include (1) allowing attackers to change sides when either reaches eight points and to bring their points with them, which should even out any imbalance of setter skill levels, or (2) having the setters compete within the game by switching sides when the first designated attacker (left, middle, or right) reaches eight

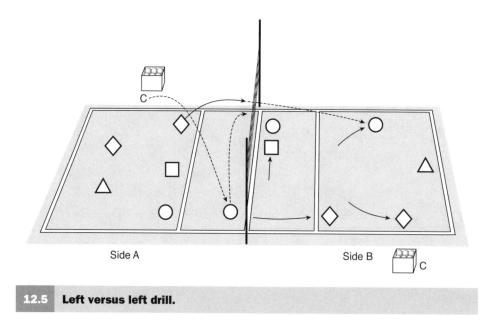

Side A   Side B

12.5 **Left versus left drill.**

points, and bringing their points with them and tracking additional points throughout the remainder of the game, so that each setter could compare total points.

LIBERO VERSUS LIBERO

Building on the 4v4 version of this drill in chapter 8 (figure 8.7), now we create a 6v6 competition. Two teams of six players are on each side of the court in specialized court positions (figure 12.6). A ball basket is placed near each endline, and half of the court on each side of the net is outlined using hot spot floor markers. On each play one libero will be required to serve to the opposing libero in that zone. Any serve landing outside of the designated zone is a point for the receiving libero. The libero winning a rally in this drill can choose whether they want to initiate the next play by serving at the opposing libero, or instead, they can choose to put the opposing libero in the serving role. The libero in the second scenario allows their serve receive skills to be on display but will still rely on their teammates to put the ball away and help them earn points. To nullify differences in the ability levels on each side of the net, when either libero reaches 13, the liberos switch sides and bring their points with them. Setters can set to any attacker throughout rallies. Whenever

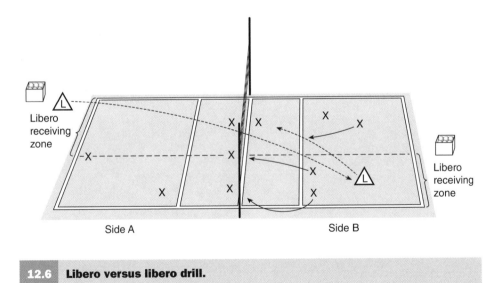

Libero receiving zone

Libero receiving zone

Side A

Side B

12.6 Libero versus libero drill.

a ball cart is emptied, pause the drill while all players chase and fill the ball carts, then play continues. The game ends when a libero earns 25 points.

You can modify this drill by (1) limiting or emphasizing attack options, (2) requiring the libero to take every free ball, or (3) establishing a risk-reward bonus system where attackers hitting into the libero's playing zone get two points for a kill or minus one if the libero's successful dig leads to a successive set and swing for a point.

Modified Games

To enhance the learning process, the game of volleyball and many of the drills presented could easily be modified based on the number of participants, courts, and available floor space. Creating smaller courts puts greater emphasis on ball control, whereas limiting the number of players on either side of the net forces players to cover more court space and increase each player's opportunities to contact the ball.

Game rules could be relaxed to allow unlimited contacts in the interest of keeping the ball in play, or the rules could be tightened by limiting contacts to increase the focus on one specific skill. Practice opportunities can be enhanced for young children by lowering the net and using standard-size volleyballs that are lighter in weight. Additional benefits are small sided games for those who only have one to three people to play with and for those who are preparing for doubles competition and need to experience covering a lot of space and using different formations. There are endless benefits to making adjustments to your practices in order to refine skill development. Use these ideas and the following examples to get you thinking on how to maximize your available resources as you continue to improve your game.

Doubles Anyone?

Doubles is probably the most common modification. It is the foundation for beach volleyball as a professional sport and, beginning in 1996, as an Olympic Games sport. The emergence of sand volleyball for collegiate women as the 90th NCAA-sponsored championship in 2016 is the latest signal of the continued popularity for two-on-two competition. Let's look at a typical doubles offense.

To cover the entire court, a doubles team splits the court during serve receive. One player begins near court zone 1 and the other player near court zone 5. Servers often try to serve to court zone 6, since this will split the two players. Passers need to anticipate the direction of the serve quickly, with one player clearly signaling "mine" while the other player releases and moves to the middle of the court near the attack line (figure 13.1). This area of the court is the target area for the passer in doubles. The player receiving serve sends the ball to the target area, then prepares to attack when the partner sets the second team touch high and toward the net on the passer's side of the court.

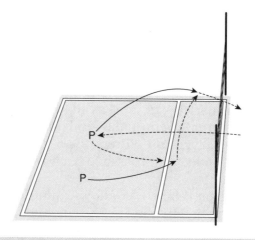

13.1 Doubles serve receive formation.

Once a doubles team mounts an attack, they need to transition to defensive positions. If the level of play results in a strong attack from an opponent, one defender should remain at the net to block, leaving the other player to cover the rest of the court. The blocker should indicate an attempt to block the line or crosscourt area so the defender can move to cover the exposed area of the court. At the moment of service, blockers can use hand signals, with one finger indicating a line block (figure 13.2a) as a signal for the defending teammate to cover the crosscourt attack. Two fingers indicating a crosscourt block (figure 13.2b) would signal the teammate to move and cover attacks being channeled down the line.

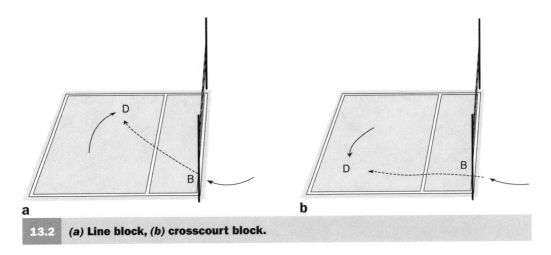

a   b

13.2 *(a) Line block, (b) crosscourt block.*

If the level of play does not result in strong attacks, both players should share responsibility for half of the court on defense, just as they would in serve receive (see figure 13.1).

If a smaller court is used, players can play in a tandem formation, with one player at the net ready to set and one player covering all of the space as a passer (figure 13.3). Once the team goes on defense, the setter stays at the net to block and the passer covers the rest of the space as a digger.

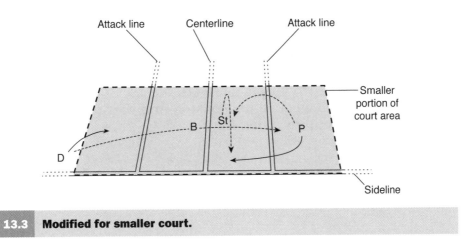

13.3 **Modified for smaller court.**

Now that we have taken a look at the doubles game, let's go over the court positions and responsibilities in other games organized for fewer than six players.

THREE ON THREE

In triples, a team uses a modified doubles format and adds a designated net player to serve as the primary setter and blocker on each play. This results in a triangle formation (figure 13.4). The other two players can serve primarily as passers, diggers, and attackers.

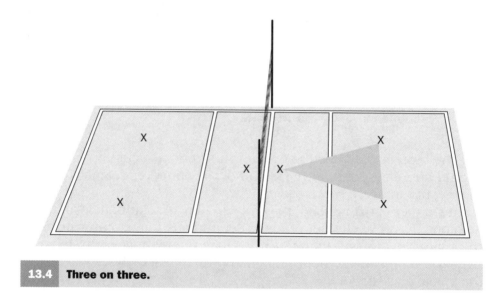

13.4 Three on three.

FOUR ON FOUR

Adding one more player to the court creates a diamond formation (figure 13.5). The fourth player moves to the deep part of the court and is primarily responsible for passing and digging. This player could also attack from the back row.

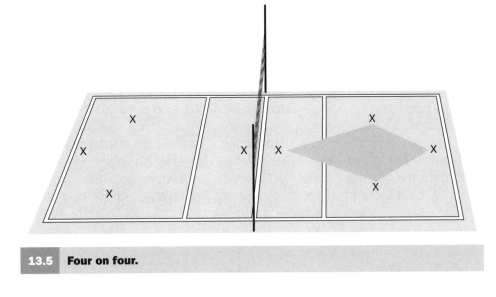

FIVE ON FIVE

When playing with five players, it's best to go back to the offensive formations discussed in chapter 11 and simply play without the right back player (figure 13.6). This adaptation minimizes the changes necessary to play since you still have three front-row players. Using a modified 4-2 style of play, simply require the two back-row players to cover a little more court space than they would in a six-on-six game.

When teams have fewer than 12 available players for practice due to injuries, a second five-on-five option on many six-on-six drills is to play without a middle front player on each side of the net. A good example is the left versus left drill in the previous chapter. This adjustment enables each attacker to swing against a single block throughout the drill.

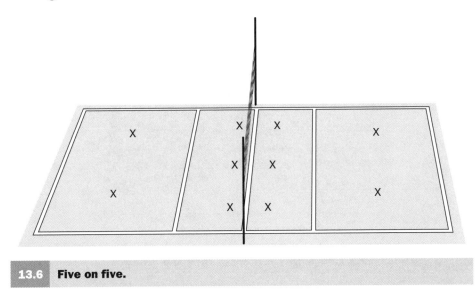

13.6   **Five on five.**

ONE-ON-ONE GAMES

Any number of scoring systems and modified rules can be used in one-on-one games. As shown in figure 13.7a, two partners could play using forearm passing cooperatively by attempting to successfully get the ball over the net 10 times in a row without an error. This one-touch game could be altered with two rule changes: (1) exclusive use of overhead passing to replace forearm passing, and (2) moving from a cooperative drill to a competitive game to 11 points.

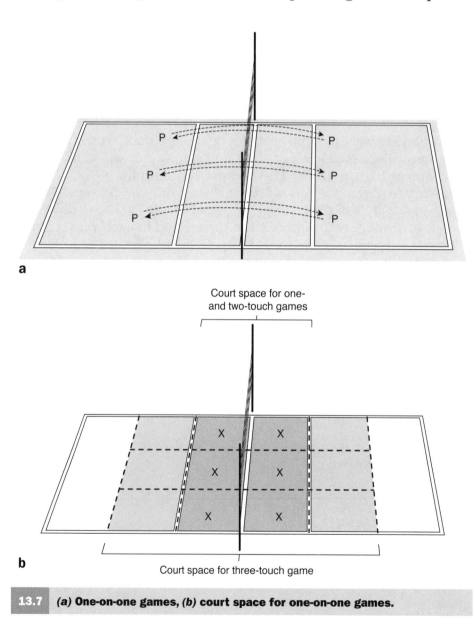

13.7 *(a)* **One-on-one games,** *(b)* **court space for one-on-one games.**

A natural progression or extension of this game is to add a second allowable touch on each side of the net: Players could be restricted by receiving the first touch with the forearms; then a second touch would be required but limited to an overhead pass across the net. The next modification for a one-on-one game is to allow, but not require, three contacts for a player each time the ball crosses the net with the restriction that no jumping is allowed, so the only legal attack would be a down ball.

Finally, a one-on-one game allowing up to three contacts for each player, each time the ball comes to their side of the net, could be changed to include a jump and swing.

See figure 13.7*b* as a reference for how to modify your available court space. Note that for all of these games, players will need to determine in advance if each rally is initiated with a toss across the net or a serve.

TWO-ON-TWO SETTING

Looking for an instant warm-up activity? Divide the court in half lengthwise and form four teams of two players (figure 13.8). Each team works together within a quarter of the court. As the ball crosses the net, a player calls for the ball as the other teammate releases and moves toward the attack area. The receiver sets the ball to the other teammate, who sets the ball over the net beyond the opponent's attack line. The teams set the ball back and forth until someone makes an error.

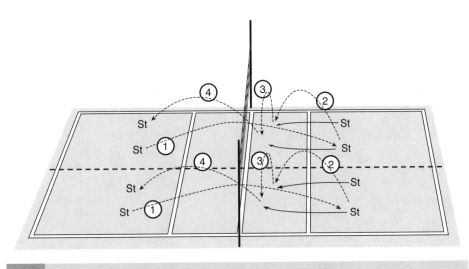

13.8 Two-on-two setting drill.

QUEEN/KING OF THE COURT

This might be the most common volleyball activity of all, especially if players are choosing a drill. Teams of three players begin on both side A and side B (figure 13.9). Two or more additional teams stand on the endline of side A. The server on side A initiates the rally. If side A wins the rally, they get a point and race around the poles to side B. Side B retrieves the ball and quickly moves outside the court to the lines forming behind side A. The next team of three steps onto side A. If side B wins the rally, they get a point and remain in place to compete against the next group of three players moving on to side A to once again initiate the next rally with a serve. Each team keeps track of its own points. The drill ends when one team reaches 15 points.

Depending on the age and experience level of the players, the serve could be eliminated and each play could start with a toss to side B.

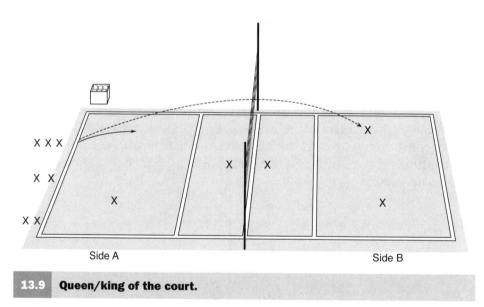

Side A   Side B

13.9 **Queen/king of the court.**

DOUBLES TOURNAMENT

It's time for a competitive two-on-two tournament. If possible, use three courts (figure 13.10). This allows 6 teams (12 players) to compete at the same time—2 teams on each court with any additional teams at the endline of each court getting ready to play. You can modify this drill based on the number of courts and participants. Each game is played to seven points.

On court one, players are required to comply with only two rules: no net violations and the serve must initiate from the endline. On court two, a rule is added—a minimum of two team contacts must be used by each team every time the ball crosses the net. On court three, three team contacts are required each time the ball crosses the net. On courts two and three, a block does not count as a team contact for the blocking team; however, an attacking team that has a ball returned from a block must restart their count for team contacts.

There is an exception to the two- and three-contact rules. One team contact is allowed on any court if a player can jump and attack the team's first team contact from a ball that crosses near the net.

Players on each team keep track of the number of games they win. Teams that win a game move to the end of the line on the next court, moving to the right. A team that wins on court three moves to the endline of court three or stays on the court if only one team is waiting on the endline. Teams that lose a game move to the end-

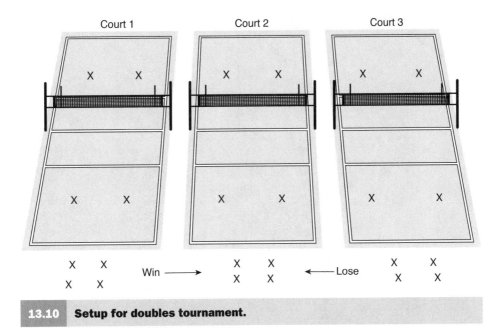

13.10 Setup for doubles tournament.

line of the next court to their left. A team that loses on court one moves to the endline of court one. The tournament continues for a designated time period. Each team reports its total wins at the end of the tournament.

REVERSE COED DOUBLES

Play using a women's-height net. Coed teams of two are formed on each available court (figure 13.11). Reverse coed rules allow women to attack at the net. Men are allowed to attack only from behind the attack line. Use this version of the drill to grow accustomed to the rules and develop some teamwork. Two teams begin on the court with a tosser stationed next to the sideline near zone 5 on side B. Another coed team helps collect volleyballs. The team on side A receives six tosses in a row. The tosser alternates tossing to the male and female player on the team. The receiving team follows reverse coed rules on each play and uses three contacts to return the ball to side B. The side B players follow reverse coed rules throughout the rally. At the end of each rally, a ball is tossed to the side A team. After six attempts, the side A players become ball collectors, the side B players move to side A, and the ball collectors move to side B.

Once you have gained some confidence, make this drill more game-like by playing a simple round-robin tournament with the three teams. Each play starts with a serve, and games are scored based on a predetermined number of points.

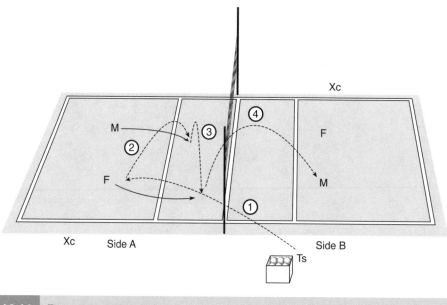

13.11 Reverse coed doubles.

Scoring Systems

For many years, traditional scoring in volleyball meant that only the serving team could score points. The first team to earn 15 points won the game, although they needed to win by 2 points. Winning a match required winning a series of games; historically, this was a best-of-three series.

The sport of volleyball has changed considerably just in the past few decades. At most competitive levels, best-of-three matches have been replaced with best-of-five matches. The term *games* has been replaced with *sets*, and rally scoring (a point is scored on every rally), which initially was used only for the deciding fifth set, is now used for the entire match.

The scoring changes, along with the introduction of the libero (see chapter 8), have been as significant as any of the new rules. Many, if not most, of the rule changes have been driven by international volleyball issues related to marketing the sport, for example, making the game more user-friendly to the television industry. Under previous rules, live television coverage of a match could require anywhere from an hour to two and a half hours.

Timed games have been used, most often with the outdoor beach game. This is an effective way to establish a definitive starting and ending point for a match.

In some cases, the idea of capping a game has been used. A capped game allows a team to win by a one-point margin.

Bonus scoring has also been tried. Bonus scoring uses traditional scoring, except the serving team scores two points when they serve and win a rally. The nonserving team scores one point if they win the rally.

The rally scoring format at one time extended the total points needed for victory to 30 points at some levels, but settled back to 25 for sets 1 through 4, with 15 points used for a fifth set. One thing is clear: when people come together to play, they have to agree on the rules before they start competing.

The wide variety of scoring systems will keep drills and games exciting. The traditional point-scoring method, in which teams play to 15 points and only score in their own term of service, may provide an enjoyable alternative, but keep in mind, this can become discouraging if your team is on the wrong end of a 2-13 score.

Using Cones

Momentum describes the apparent shifts in control from one team to another. Let's look at a fun way to see the momentum changes as they occur during a game. Decide for yourself if momentum is real or not.

Two teams of six will be needed for this game. Side A will serve first to get things started, and teams will rotate each time they are the receiving team and win a rally to earn the next serve. The drill begins with five cones several steps off the court beyond one of the poles. At the end of the first rally, the winning team moves a cone to their side of the court, a few steps away from their attack line. Notice the cones that have been added on the sideline; this is the visible scoreboard. Side B started this play with three cones on their side. A cone moves back to the middle when a team with cones loses a rally, as shown in figure 14.1 (with side A celebrating).

A team must get all five cones to their side to win the game but can only add them to their sideline if and when all cones or remaining cones are in the middle. If a team wins three cones, then loses the next six plays, this way of scoring shows what loss of momentum looks like. The team on the brink of losing (side A was losing 0-3) sees the tide turning (figure 14.2) as the cones start showing up on their side of the court (side A now leads 3-0).

14.1   Use cones as a scoreboard.

14.2   Momentum shift clearly illustrated.

Using Points

Points are the most common way of scoring games and drills. At times, you may want to award points only for successful execution of a particular skill. For example, if you want to emphasize back-row attacking, you could play a game in which a point is scored only when a team ends a rally with a back-row attack. Or you could use the bonus scoring idea and award three points to the team that successfully executes a back-row attack but only one point to the team that wins the rally any other way. This type of competition can get very exciting in a hurry; the team that is behind has the chance to catch up quickly by going for bonus points.

Activation

Late in my coaching career, I came across activation, although, like most drills I used, I cannot recall where I first saw this activity. Building on the example in chapter 12 (figure 12.4), the scoreboard in this activity is activated when either team scores on a back-row attack. That team would then receive free balls consecutively until the opponent wins a rally.

In figure 14.3, side A has scored on a back-row attack and their scoreboard is now activated. The coach on side B will bounce a ball into that side, who must give a free ball to the activated opponent. If side A scores (in any manner) on this rally, they would receive a point, and the coach on side B would bounce another ball high into side B's court. That team would again be required to send a free ball to side A. The activated team accumulates points until they lose a rally, and the scoreboard is deactivated. Side A should initiate the next play with a serve, which would provide side B with the first opportunity to score on a back-row attack, earn activation, and get some points on their side of the scoreboard.

Wondering how else could you use this in a practice session? Here's an example. If a team has been introducing the slide attack to their middle hitters but players have been hesitant to use that tactic in recent matches, make scoring on a slide the criteria for activation during practice; both teams will be highly motivated to execute that skill. Multiple criteria can also be used in this drill. For example, teams could be activated either for scoring on a back-row attack or

14.3 *(a)* Side A scores on back-row attack, scoreboard activated, *(b)* coach bounces ball to side B, *(c)* activated side A receives free ball, *(d)* side A scores first point and will receive another free ball.

a slide. Your team isn't serving tough enough? Activate for every ace serve. Want to teach your lefty opposite to run a front slide? Activate a team when the opposite in right front scores on a 52 when they travel from court zone 2 to court zone 3. The possibilities are endless for this drill.

Wave Rotation

During a game, players rotate in a clockwise direction. In a drill or scrimmage game, players can rotate in several ways. One effective method of rotating is wave rotation (figure 14.4).

Think of the endline on side A as the ocean and the endline on side B as the shore. The waves move from side A to side B. This is a fun way to rotate players. The queen/king of the court drill (figure 13.9) uses wave rotation.

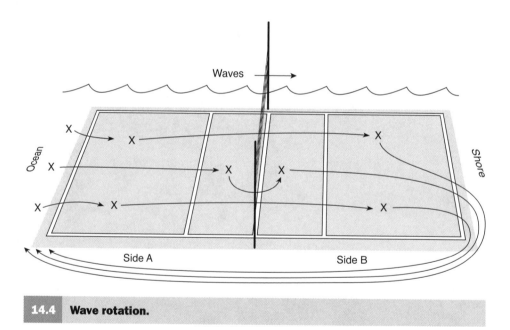

14.4　**Wave rotation.**

Wash Drills

One last scoring system that has gained incredible popularity is the wash method of scoring drills. For example, in a six-on-six game, each team serves once (figure 14.7). If the same team wins both rallies, that team wins a point and gets to rotate. If the teams split the rallies, they wash each other out and the drill begins again. A team can win only when they have rotated six times, back to where they began. Instead of playing for points, each team plays for the chance to rotate. Instead of playing to 15 points, as in traditional scoring, each team essentially plays to 6 points.

This is an effective way for new learners to practice. If several rallies end up in a wash, players get to practice the same position for several rallies in a row. For example, a server who is struggling may get several chances to serve before either team wins a rotation. Furthermore, a team ahead on the scoreboard could easily get stuck in a rotation, and the opponent could get back in the game.

How about if a team has starters practicing against reserves? Double up the challenge for first teamers by adjusting the criteria to rotate with a three-rally sequence in which starters serve, receive, and then serve again. The second team can rotate if they win two of the three rallies, and starters earn a rotation only when they win all three plays. A wash in this modification occurs when starters win two out of three.

Wash scoring is also effective in a transition drill. Instead of serving each time, players could receive a free ball each time they win a rally. The bonus ball drill (figure 9.13) is an example of a transition wash drill. In that drill, it's a wash if neither team wins their bonus ball.

— *Give it a go* —

FOUR-ON-FOUR WAVE

Building on the queen/king of the court drill from chapter 13 (figure 13.9), add in a fourth player as a front-row setter (and blocker) and require all attacks to come from the back row. Two groups of four players begin on each side of the net (figure 14.5), with an additional team of four behind the side A endline. It would be wise to add a whistle from a coach or players out of practice with injuries each time a back-row attacker jumps with any part of their foot on or in front of the attack line. Side A players serve for five consecutive plays, then that group waves to side B. Side B waves off the court, collects volleyballs, then lines up behind the side A endline. The team behind the side A endline takes the court and serves for the next five plays. All teams track their score until the first team reaches 25.

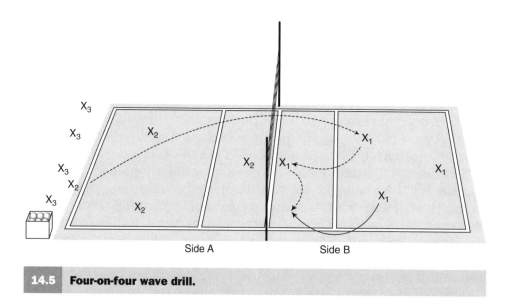

14.5 **Four-on-four wave drill.**

SIX-ON-SIX WAVE

Figure 14.6 is ideal to help beginning players get a feel for every position on the court. Side B back-row players (labeled as X_i) receive a toss over the net from side A on each play. Once each of the three side B back-row players has taken one of those three tosses to initiate a rally, the wave takes them off the court (to the shore), and they return outside of the court behind side A. Three new players from

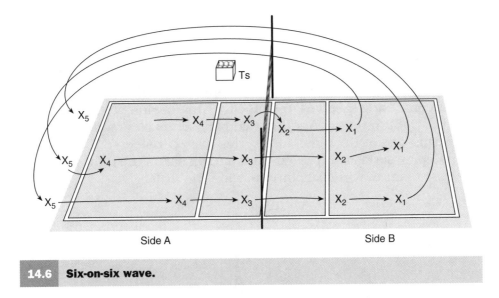

14.6   Six-on-six wave.

side A (labeled as X_5) enter play now, and for the next three plays they start each rally playing back-row defense. (Let's follow them as the wave moves them forward.) In the next sequence, they would now play as front-row defenders to start the next three rallies, then the wave goes around the poles, and they become front-row attackers for three plays. Eventually, the wave takes them to the side B back row, where each of them will get one of the three free balls tossed across the net, and they start each rally in back-row offense. So now as we follow them off the court (to the shore), when they run back to re-form a line behind side A endline, whoever entered the last time in court zone 1 would enter in court zone 6, whoever entered in court zone 6 enters now in court zone 5, and the player who had entered last time in court zone 5 enters in court zone 1. Essentially, as illustrated here, once all 18 players wave through three times, each person would have played three rallies in every single spot on the court. It is a great way to get comfortable with the game.

SIX-ON-SIX WASH

This is a good way to emphasize the importance of winning two rallies in a row. Two teams of six begin on the court (figure 14.7). The teams complete a two-play series. Side A serves first. Regardless of the outcome, side B serves next. If either team wins both plays, they earn the right to rotate. Another two-play series commences. If each team wins one of the plays in a series, it is considered a wash and the two-play series is repeated until a team earns the right to rotate. The first team to win six rotations wins the drill.

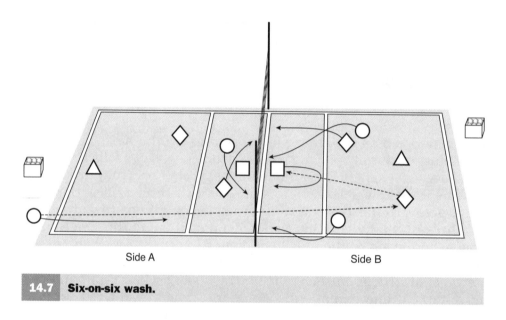

Side A   Side B

14.7   **Six-on-six wash.**

About the Author

Joel B. Dearing retired after the 2010 season from a 30-year and 40-season (combining women's and men's teams) collegiate coaching career with an overall 899-384 record. Dearing was the first coach for the women's and men's programs at Roger Williams University before taking over both programs at Springfield College in Massachusetts in 1989. He finished with a 728-310 career record and .701 winning percentage for his women's teams, putting him in the top 10 in NCAA Division III history. His 1996 Springfield College men's team was undefeated against Division III competition and finished the season ranked first in the country. He remains on the Springfield College faculty, teaching full time in the athletic administration graduate program.

Dearing is a member of the American Volleyball Coaches Association (AVCA) and a member of USA Volleyball's cadre of coaches. He is a five-time recipient of the AVCA Region Coach of the Year Award (1993, 1994, 1996, 2003, and 2008), was honored by the International Volleyball Hall of Fame with the Mintonette Medallion of Merit Award in 2013, and was elected into the Springfield College Athletic Hall of Fame in 2015. He is also the author of *The Untold Story of William G. Morgan—Inventor of Volleyball.*

Dearing Leadership LLC was established in 2018 and includes Dearing Volleyball School (started in 1984), where he runs his summer camps and coaching clinics. Dearing also conducts leadership training seminars and is available for motivational and public speaking engagements.